Text SAVERIO VILLA

Rendering MARCO DE FABIANIS MANFERTO

2–3 • Ferrari P4/5 by Pininfarina.

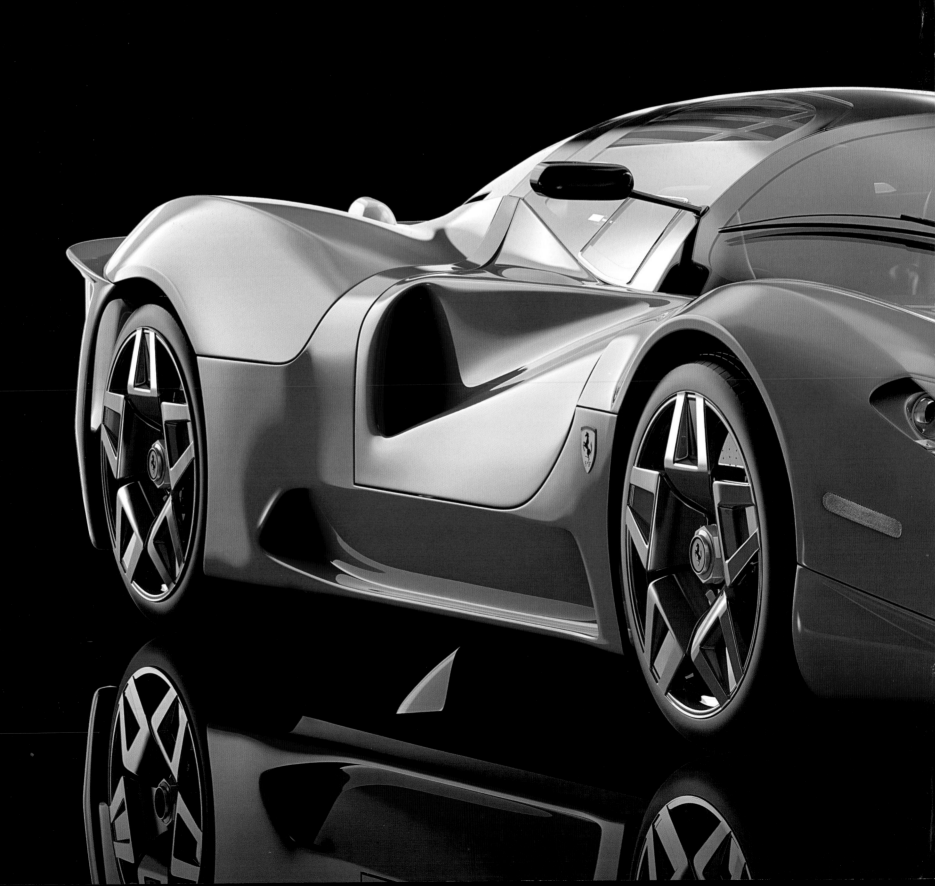

FERRARI

MEET THE LEGEND

Contents

4 AND 6–7 • TWO VIEWS OF THE FERRARI LaFERRARI.

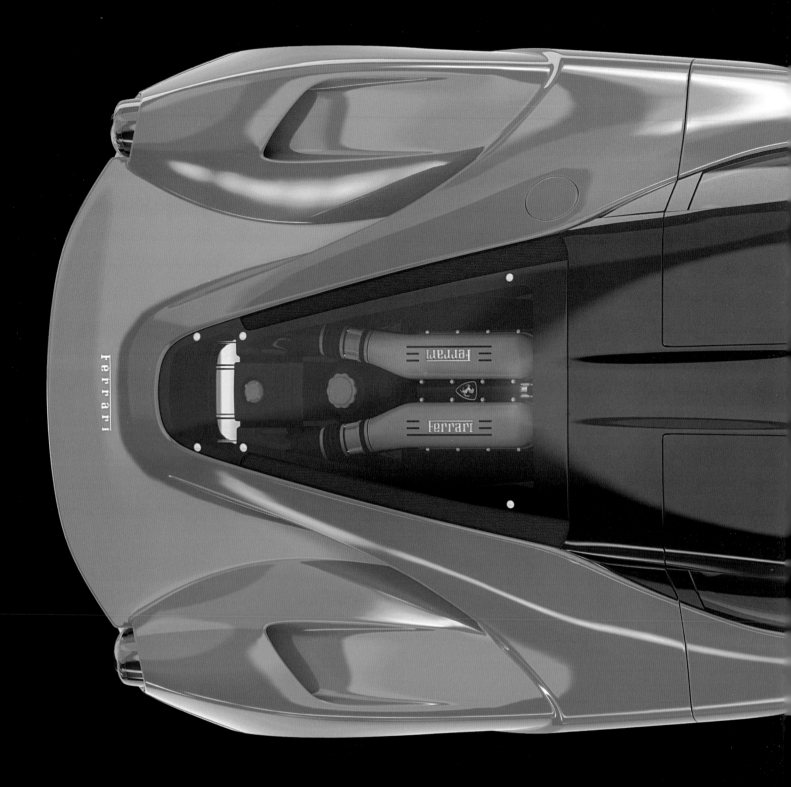

The myth that goes beyond the car

It is not necessary to be an automobile fan to know and love Ferrari, because Ferrari is part of the history of the modern world. It is a multifaceted myth linking the idea of the automobile: the evolution of technology, design, and culture. The Maranello company is the protagonist of an epoch filled with unbeatable racing cars, desperate challenges on the most difficult tracks in the world, and unequaled road cars. There are also so many stories of men who have made the Prancing Horse great, together with the "Grand Old

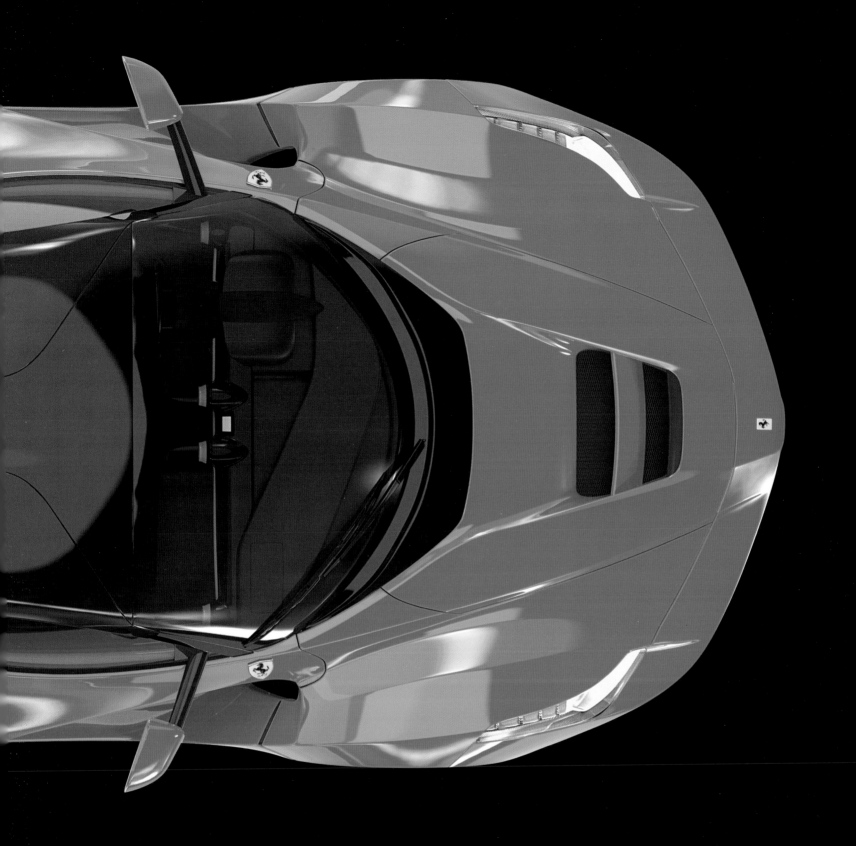

Man," perhaps in conflict with him, and also after his death. Ferrari moved from being a small, enthusiastic provincial company at the end of the Second World War to being a world phenomenon in technology, image, marketing, and value; it has become, according to experts, "the strongest brand in the world."

It is just for this reason that this new edition of the book has added a chapter dedicated to the unforgettable figures at Maranello and one relating the history of Ferrari linked to that of Formula One, which has made and continues to make a crucial contribution to the myth of the Prancing Horse. Of course, in addition to the faithful reconstruction of its history, which began in 1947, the volume includes the designs, technical analysis, and specifications of the most important Ferrari models, from the 166 Inter of 1948 to the incredible hybrid SF90 Stradale of 2019. The result is a work that guides the reader through time—a fascinating journey through cars, races, anecdotes, and lives.

· From the workshop in Modena to quotation on Wall Str

the workshop in Modena to quotation on Wall Street · I

workshop in Modena to quotation on Wall Street · From tl

shop in Modena to quotation on Wall Street · From the worl

Modena to quotation on Wall Street · From the workshop in M

to quotation on Wall Street · From the workshop in Modena to

Modena to quotati

to quotation on Wal

on on Wall Street ·

/all Street · From t

From the workshop in Modena to quotation on Wall Street

the workshop in Modena to quotation on Wall Street · FROM THE WOR

shop in Modena to quotation on Wall Street · FROM THE WORKSHOP

Modena to quotation on Wall Street · FROM THE WORKSHOP IN MOD

to quotation on Wall Street · FROM THE WORKSHOP IN MODENA TO

tation on Wall Street · FROM THE WORKSHOP IN MODENA TO QUOT

on Wall Street · FROM THE WORKSHOP IN MODENA TO QUOTATION

Street · FROM THE WORKSHOP IN MODENA TO QUOTATION ON WA

ET • From the workshop in Modena to quotation on Wall Street • FROM

om the workshop in Modena to quotation on Wall Street • FROM THE

workshop in Modena to quotation on Wall Street • FROM THE WORK-

hop in Modena to quotation on Wall Street • FROM THE WORKSHOP IN

dena to quotation on Wall Street • FROM THE WORKSHOP IN MODENA

otation on Wall Street • FROM THE WORKSHOP IN MODENA TO QUO-

on Wall Street • FROM THE WORKSHOP IN MODENA TO QUOTATION

treet • FROM THE WORKSHOP IN MODENA TO QUOTATION ON WALL

OM THE WORKSHOP IN MODENA TO QUOTATION ON WALL STREET

E WORKSHOP IN MODENA TO QUOTATION ON WALL STREET • From

HOP IN MODENA TO QUOTATION ON WALL STREET • From the work-

MODENA TO QUOTATION ON WALL STREET • From the workshop in

A TO QUOTATION ON WALL STREET • From the workshop in Modena

JOTATION ON WALL STREET • From the workshop in Modena to quo-

ION ON WALL STREET • From the workshop in Modena to quotation

WALL STREET • From the workshop in Modena to quotation on Wall

STREET • From the workshop in Modena to quotation on Wall Street •

Ferrari. A legendary name. A unique story. No other automobile marque in the world has ever been so closely associated with the name and personality of its founder. The heart and soul of the Prancing Horse marque. Enzo Ferrari. Born in Modena, Italy, in 1898, the young Enzo's first contact with mechanical engineering was in the workshop of his father, Alfredo.

Later in life he was to earn the nickname "Drake," in honor of Sir Francis Drake, the Elizabethan privateer who defeated the invincible Spanish Armada with the English fleet in 1588—and also in recognition of Enzo's outstanding ability throughout his life to make the seemingly impossible possible. His early years were not easy. In 1915 his father and brother Alfredo, known as Dino, died in quick succession. Enzo himself contracted pleurisy and was honorably discharged from military service in the Italian Royal Army. At the end of World War I, Ferrari applied for a job at Fiat but was refused. In 1920 he nevertheless started racing with Alfa Romeo and several years later won the first edition of the Gran Premio del Circuito del Savio at the racetrack near Ravenna. One of those present was the mother of Francesco Baracca, a WWI fighter ace and holder of the gold medal of military valor. She presented Ferrari with the Prancing Horse emblem originally painted on the fuselage of her late son's plane. Her advice to Ferrari was to affix the emblem to his cars as a mascot.

The emblem thus became the symbol of the Maranello marque, setting a milestone in automotive history that day.

In 1929, completely recovered from a serious case of nervous exhaustion, Enzo Ferrari was called to Milan to found a race team managed by Alfa Romeo, a team destined to become the widely celebrated Scuderia Ferrari. Strongly driven by his dreams, often visionary and obsessive, Ferrari persuaded the well-established car designer Vittorio Jano to leave Fiat and join the Scuderia.

10–11 • YOUNG ENZO FERRARI (FAR RIGHT) WITH THE ALFA ROMEO TEAM, WHICH HE MANAGED BEFORE HE FOUNDED HIS OWN COMPANY. IN THE CENTER IS NICOLA ROMEO, WHO PURCHASED ALFA IN 1918.

Monza 1923

Initially, the Drake was not only the founder and director of the team, but also a team driver. Ferrari himself continued racing until 1932, when his son Dino was born. Dino was named in memory of Enzo's late brother Alfredino. A whole string of victories arrived, win after win. The Scuderia Ferrari grew steadily in size, eventually employing over forty drivers, including such famous names as Antonio Ascari, Giuseppe Campari, and Tazio Nuvolari. In effect, it went from being the racing branch of a car maker to an independent team in its own right. Alfa Romeo, somewhat startled by such success, tried everything to keep the Commendatore, the title awarded to Enzo as early as 1927, tied to its brand name. Its efforts included appointing Ferrari Director of Sports at the Alfa Corse racing department.

This was an extraordinary success story for a person who was neither an engineer, a designer, nor a professional manager. In 1939, after ten years with Alfa Romeo, Enzo Ferrari left the company following irreconcilable differences with Alfa management. In 1940, using his severance pay, Ferrari founded the Auto Avio Costruzioni company in Modena. His workshops there produced two spiders built mainly with Fiat components.

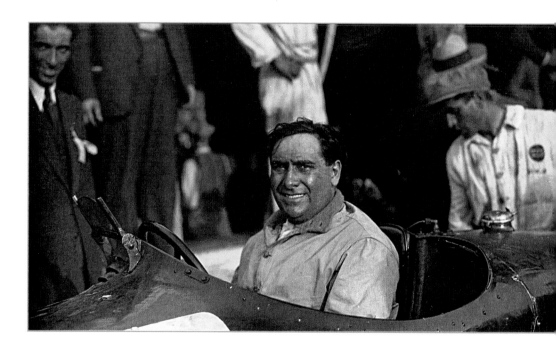

12 • TAZIO NUVOLARI AND HIS ALFA WITH THE PRANCING HORSE BADGE, IN NICE IN 1935. ENZO FERRARI WAS GIVEN PERMISSION TO USE THE BADGE BY FRANCESCO BARACCA'S MOTHER.

13 TOP • ALBERTO ASCARI DRIVING HIS FERRARI 125 TO VICTORY IN THE DAILY EXPRESS TROPHY RACE AT SILVERSTONE IN 1949, FINISHING AHEAD OF FARINA AND VILLORESI.

13 CENTER • TAZIO NUVOLARI IN HIS ALFA ROMEO 12C, MANAGED BY THE SCUDERIA FERRARI, DURING THE 1936 VANDERBILT CUP ON THE LONG ISLAND CIRCUIT.

13 BOTTOM • GIUSEPPE CAMPARI IN HIS ALFA 8C 2300. THIS CAR, DRIVEN BY TAZIO NUVOLARI, WON THE 1931 ITALIAN GP, BEATING BUGATTI, MERCEDES, TALBOT, AND MASERATI.

The success of these vehicles was linked primarily to the smooth, flowing lines of the two-seater bodywork powered by a 91.5 cu in (1,500 cc) eight-cylinder engine. The body was built by the Carrozzeria Touring coachworks in Milan and was inspired by the 1939 Alfa Romeo 6C 2500 SS. The Milanese coachworks was also known by its trade name "Touring Superleggera" (Touring Superlightweight) after the construction method, introduced in 1936, which combined a thin tubular steel chassis-frame with aluminum body panels.

Everything seemed to be set for new triumphs. Ferrari had set up on his own, fulfilling the dream of a lifetime. But everything changed with the outbreak of the Second World War. All race events were cancelled, and industry was obliged to change over to war production. This was a cruel blow to the Drake's dreams. The Auto Avio Costruzioni started to produce grinding machines for making ball bearings. Toward the end of the war, fighting and bombing began to threaten Modena. The company was transferred from Modena to a site in the countryside at Maranello just 12 miles (19 km) away. This was to become the headquarters of the Ferrari marque.

When the war ended, Enzo Ferrari, once free of the contractual restrictions imposed by Alfa Romeo, started to harbor the idea of creating a car which would carry his name. He resumed his ties with trusted colleagues from his Alfa Romeo days, including technician Giuseppe Busso, tester Luigi Bazzi, and designer Gioacchino Colombo. Colombo was given the task of producing the first real Ferrari, dated 1947. The car, called the 125 S, was powered by a longitudinal, front-mounted 91.5 cu in (1.5 liter) V12.

The 125 S therefore had to be a modern state-of-the-art winner. The car met expectations. After only five months, it had won six of the fourteen competition events in which it had been entered. The Ferrari legend was born. The car was immediately put on sale, and those who wanted to race the 125 S could also benefit from works logistic and technical support. The year 1948 was crucial. The Drake wanted to start production of a competition vehicle for the Sports category.

The result was the 166 MM Touring, where the initials MM stand for Mille Miglia. This roadster was powered by a front-mounted 60° V12 with a displacement of 122 cu in (1,995 cc) and is credited with having 140 hp. Needless to say, it attracted immediate interest and admiration. The stiffening rib running along the body sides between the front and rear wheel arches defined the 166 MM as a barchetta, a name used from that time onward to describe the bodywork style of all the Maranello spiders.

The year 1951 marked a turning point in the fortunes of the Maranello marque. The British Grand Prix at Silverstone was won by the Argentinian driver José Froilán González driving a Ferrari 375 F1, finishing ahead of a strong Alfa Romeo team. This was Ferrari's first win in F1 Grand Prix racing, a historic triumph which was to mark the opening of a new era for the Prancing Horse marque.

The echo of Ferrari's success was heard across the Atlantic. The Drake immediately recognized the importance of internationalizing his brand, and appointed driver Luigi Chinetti, founder of the North American Racing Team (NART), as exclusive importer of Ferrari cars in the United States. Once again Ferrari's instinct proved right, and the U.S. soon became one of the most important markets for the Prancing Horse marque.

In 1951, Enzo Ferrari was the first to toast the opening of the Carrozzeria Scaglietti coachworks. Carrozzeria Scaglietti in Modena was founded by Sergio Scaglietti, a Scuderia veteran from the Alfa Romeo days who still worked with Ferrari. The Scaglietti coachworks immediately became a vital component of the "Made in Maranello" marque, with the Modena works providing the bodies for Ferrari grand touring models.

Highly memorable examples of Scaglietti's art were the two barchettas, the 250 California LWB and the 250 Testa Rossa, and the 250 GTO Berlinetta. The collaboration between the two companies continued smoothly and without interruption for over twenty years. In 1975, Ferrari bought the majority shareholding in the Carrozzeria Scaglietti, which then became an integral part of the Ferrari organization.

Scaglietti was a wizard with sheet aluminum. But what Ferrari needed now was a designer. To find one, he had to look further afield, to Turin. Turin was the capital of Italy's Piedmont region and also the birthplace of Battista Farina. Battista Farina was nicknamed "Pinin," local dialect for the name Giuseppino and also indicating that he was the youngest/smallest member of the Farina industrial family. From when the two first met, the collaboration between the Maranello marque and the Turin design house has produced over a hundred models designed by Pininfarina. The collaboration has persisted for more than sixty years and shows no signs of waning. While the relationship with the Turin design house went from strength to strength, Enzo Ferrari had to face one of the hardest, most difficult tests of his life: the passing of his son Dino. Alfredo Ferrari, known as Dino, had been born in 1932 from Ferrari's marriage to Laura Garello. Dino was not Ferrari's only son; Enzo had another son, Piero, born in 1945 from his relationship with Lina Lardi. However, Ferrari undoubtedly saw Dino as his designated heir from day one. Dino was also a mechanical engineer of considerable talent. But he was diagnosed with muscular dystrophy and died in 1956 at the age of just 24. Enzo was devastated, deeply distraught by a grief that would mark his personal and professional life from then on.

17 • THE FERRARI "ASSEMBLY LINE" IN THE NINETEEN-SIXTIES.

At the end of the nineteen-sixties, Enzo Ferrari realized that he needed the backing of an automotive giant if he was to continue to compete at the highest levels and to find the resources needed to design and develop the road cars of the future. This would inevitably involve selling a shareholding in his company.

After contacts with Ford, initially promising but destined to failure because the American company did not intend to allow Enzo Ferrari the decision-making freedom he demanded, Ferrari was saved by the providential intervention of Gianni Agnelli and the Fiat auto company. Fiat management came to Maranello's rescue. Philanthropy? Anything but. The publicity value and the media spinoff from a joint venture with Ferrari was very advantageous to Turin-based Fiat. The Drake had won again, even though he had to cede a 50% shareholding to the Turin-based car maker in 1969. The Commendatore was nevertheless allowed complete autonomy in the management of competition activities and was also permitted access to Ferrari Industriale funds.

Here it should be noted that the finances of competition management and the production of road-going GT cars had been separated in 1964. In 1969 it was already clear to everyone that Ferrari was destined to end up under the aegis of Fiat. When Enzo Ferrari acknowledged paternity of his son Piero Lardi and registered 10% of the company's share capital in Piero's name, it was already clear that the remaining 40% was already on its way to Turin. This happened at the beginning of the nineteen-eighties.

18 • ENZO FERRARI USED TO PERSONALLY SUPERVISE THE DEVELOPMENT OF ALL HIS CARS. HERE, WE SEE HIM FROM BEHIND DURING THE TESTING OF ONE OF HIS FIRST REAR-ENGINED SINGLE-SEATERS IN 1960.

19 • THE FERRARI STAFF IN APRIL 1961 AT THE FIRST TESTING OF THE 156. IN THAT YEAR, THE FERRARI 156 WON THE F1 WORLD CHAMPIONSHIP WITH PHIL HILL. RICHIE GINTHER IS IN THE DRIVER'S SEAT.

The wide degree of autonomy that Fiat guaranteed Enzo Ferrari in the management of competition activities allowed him to dream the impossible dream: the building of a test track which would reproduce some of the most demanding sections of the main race circuits of the world. For many, this was sheer utopia. For the Commendatore, it was an objective to be pursued just like any other victory. The track was built at Fiorano, just a few miles from Maranello. The Fiorano track was built as a proving ground, initially for testing racecars and then later for road vehicles. It was a test circuit for training drivers and mechanics and in general for making the Prancing Horse teams more competitive. The Drake fell head over heels in love with the track, going so far as to build a small house for himself inside the perimeter; the office in the house where he worked has been kept for posterity.

Ferrari passed judgment thus: "From that moment onwards, no Ferrari would have to face the track or series production without first having passed the Fiorano exam with full marks." True then, and still true today.

In 1973, not long after the construction of the Fiorano track, the company underwent another sea change when Luca Cordero di Montezemolo joined Ferrari. Montezemolo was a godsend, a next-generation manager tasked at the age of just 26 with leading the Maranello company into the future. Montezemolo, assistant to Enzo Ferrari, was appointed director of the race team, and his efforts were rewarded in 1975 when Ferrari won the Formula 1 World Constructors' Championship. But Maranello was to be only the launchpad for this ambitious young manager from Bologna, who left Ferrari after only four years.

21 • AN AERIAL VIEW OF THE FIORANO PRIVATE CIRCUIT IN 1980.

The eighties were dark times for Ferrari in racing, human, and commercial terms. The first blow had already been dealt in 1977 when driver Niki Lauda decided to leave the Ferrari team. His place was taken by the Canadian Gilles Villeneuve. For Ferrari, Gilles was like a son. When he died during qualifiers for the Belgian Grand Prix in 1982, a light in Enzo Ferrari's life seemed to go out. Forever. Despite the tragedy, Maranello continued to build cars destined to become motoring legends. The first of these was the 288 GTO.

Next up was the Testarossa, a masterpiece by Pininfarina where the mechanical layout and the technical problems to overcome gave rise to innovative design features, such as the louvers to cool the rear-mounted radiators, which made this car instantly recognizable. And then there was the 400, a 2+2 flagship with delightfully clean lines. However, sales of the grand touring vehicles did not take off, and success on the racetrack seemed a long time coming. Not even the F40 could restore the serenity that the Grand Old Man sought. The car was a sensation and enjoyed a success that exceeded all expectations. Demand was such that Ferrari was "obliged" to make over 1,300 units. The F40 became a legend. This was the spiritual successor to the 288 GTO. Also designed by Pininfarina, it had a raw, mean look and was the last supercar to be made under the Drake's management. Enzo Ferrari passed away on August 14, 1988, at the age of 90.

In accordance with his wishes, news of his death was not announced until after the burial ceremony. He was buried alongside his beloved son Dino. Just a few months before his death, he said of himself: "I am someone who dreamed of becoming Ferrari." Enzo Ferrari, the Grand Old Man, was no more.

Just as the dark clouds seemed to gather over Maranello, now deprived of its leader, an old acquaintance returned to disperse the gloom—Luca Cordero di Montezemolo. It was 1991, twelve years since the Prancing Horse marque had won anything in the World Formula One Championship. The turnaround in competition fortunes came with the appointment of Jean Todt as general manager, the first non-Italian to lead the Scuderia, and the signing of a world-class driver, the unbeatable Michael Schumacher. In 2000, Ferrari returned to winning form with the German ace in the Drivers' Championship and also in the Constructor's Championship. In the meantime, cars like the 355 and the 360 Modena had taken sales figures back into the black. This was due to continuous technical development and the maintenance of a certain stylistic continuity in the designs by Pininfarina. The 355 Berlinetta saw the debut on a road car of an aerodynamic undertray designed to create ground effect. The approach was consistent but certainly nontraditional. The 360 Modena, for example, broke all the design canons of the time. It saw the introduction of a new styling approach at Ferrari inspired by the ancient, omnipotent divinity—aerodynamics.

This was clear evidence that the company now had its crisis behind it—even to the point of thinking about expanding. This it did in 1997, when Fiat acquired Maserati.

22 • MICHAEL SCHUMACHER HUGGING HIS GOOD FRIEND JEAN TODT, FERRARI SPORTING DIRECTOR, AFTER WINNING THE SAN MARINO GP ON MAY 2, 1999.

Maserati had been Ferrari's traditional rival, challenged thousands of times on race circuits throughout the world.

Enzo Ferrari's transformation from driver to sports director and car maker had been prompted by his friend and rival Adolfo Orsi, one-time proprietor of the Trident marque. Now Maserati was to become part of the Maranello organization. It remained there until 2005, when it returned to Fiat. In 1997, Ferrari built its own wind tunnel, a masterpiece designed by the world-famous architect Renzo Piano. The building resembles a mechanical component of an engine rather than a building. The central element is a 262-foot-long (80 m) tubular duct, with a 14-foot-diameter (5 m) turbine fan blowing air through the duct. The airflow can be regulated to simulate a maximum speed of 155 mph (250 km/h). Enzo would have been ecstatic.

The wind tunnel was just the first part of the much wider-ranging initiative. The "Formula Uomo" project was designed to implement a radical renewal of the product facility at Maranello. Developments included a new mechanical engineering workshop for assembling Ferrari and Maserati engines. Logistics were revolutionized both for the delivery of road cars and for the movements of the race team. The principles of bioarchitecture were implemented with the inten-

tion of melding an industrial facility into its surroundings. As Monte-zemolo liked to affirm, "to build exceptional products you need exceptional people working in ideal conditions in an exceptional working environment."

The year 2002 saw the birth of the Enzo supercar. The sportscar world would never be the same again. Those who believed that the F40 and F50 had reached the pinnacle of performance in a road-legal car had to think again. The Ferrari brand had considerably in-creased its lead over rival marques. Success was to attract numerous investors from outside Italy.

24 AND 25 • THE MARANELLO WIND TUNNEL LOOKS LIKE A WORK OF ART. IT WAS DESIGNED BY ARCHITECT RENZO PIANO AND OPENED IN 1997. INSIDE THE TUNNEL, THE CAR'S AERODYNAMICS ARE ALSO DEVELOPED BY WORKING ON FULL-SCALE MODELS. ON THE LEFT, THE F300 TESTING IN 1998.

In 2006, the Mubadala Development Company of Abu Dhabi acquired a 5% shareholding in the company. Mubadala promoted the building of "Ferrari World Abu Dhabi," the first theme park in the world dedicated to an automotive brand. The F430, 599 GTB Fiorano, 458 Italia, and F12 models sold as if there were no tomorrow. Commercial success was also based on technical innovations such as all-wheel drive on the Ferrari FF. Brand image was further enhanced by the debut of the California, the first roadster with a retractable hard top. The California was a true break with the past—the first front-engined Ferrari with a V8 in the position previously reserved for the classic V12, and a dual clutch in place of the more usual F1 electro-hydraulic unit. It was also the first Ferrari with direct fuel injection. In 2012, the first Ferrari museum outside Italy was inaugurated in Shanghai, China. At the same time, Ferrari was also developing a top-class supercar with the most extreme performance ever achieved by a Maranello production car—LaFerrari. The first series hybrid from the Prancing Horse marque. Extreme like no other berlinetta. Successor to the F40, the F50, and the Enzo, and designed to project Ferrari in a new era. From a corporate standpoint, the third millennium brought considerable sporting success to Ferrari: on American soil they had important wins, with three 12 Hours of Sebring and one 24-Hour Daytona, but it was above all from Formula One that a series of significant victories came to the team: between 2000 and 2008, they won no fewer than 13 world championships—six drivers' titles (five with Michael Schumacher and one with Kimi Räikkönen), and seven constructors' titles. However, after that came the lean years.

From a commercial standpoint, these were the years that saw the launch of successful models like the Enzo in 2002, the F430 in 2004, and, above all, the start of a branding policy that, following the opening of the first Ferrari Store at Maranello in 2002, culminated in a series of openings in Italy and abroad, taking the Ferrari brand to thirty flagship stores all over the world, to cities like Saint Petersburg, Dubai, Abu Dhabi, Singapore, New York, and Miami.

In the first ten years, the team's presence was extended to emerging markets such as the Middle East, China, Japan and the rest of Asia; and its position in the U.S., UK, and Germany was consolidated.

In 2015, the Fiat Chrysler Automobile Group, formed in 2014, put up 10% of its Ferrari shares for sale; on October 21, Ferrari was quoted on the New York Stock Exchange. The following January, Ferrari was also quoted on the Italian Stock Exchange, becoming an independent company. In the meantime, the sales figures climbed, also thanks to the other models appreciated by clients, like the 488 (2015) and the Portofino (2018).

In 2018, 9,251 on-road Ferraris were produced, and finally the constant effort of reaching the target of ten thousand vehicles was at hand when the first Ferrari SUV, the Purosangue, was announced, extending the market for the Prancing Horse even further.

What is more, the 488 marked the return to supercharging, and its V8 turbo engine was elected International Engine of the Year from 2016 to 2018 and nominated the "Best of the Best" among all the winning engines of the last twenty years.

Unfortunately, in 2018, President and Managing Director Sergio Marchionne, who had taken over from Luca Cordero di Montezemolo in 2014, died unexpectedly. He had had important and ambitious plans for the Modena-based marque.

His scepter has been taken up by new President John Elkann and new CEO Louis Camilleri, who presented their plans for the company to the shareholders gathered at the new Style Center: fifteen new vehicles in three years, and a forward-looking range that will be 60% composed of hybrid models.

26 • A SATELLITE IMAGE OF THE FERRARI WORLD THEME PARK IN ABU DHABI. COVERING MORE THAN 1 MILLION SQUARE FEET (100,000 SQ M), IT WAS OPENED TO THE PUBLIC ON NOVEMBER 4, 2010.

27 • SERGIO MARCHIONNE, PRESIDENT OF FERRARI FROM 2014 TO 2018, AT THE NEW YORK STOCK EXCHANGE AFTER FCA BEGAN ITS NEW LISTING ON OCTOBER 13, 2014.

FERRARI AND FORMULA I: INTERLINKED AND INSEPARABLE DESTIN

RI AND FORMULA I: INTERLINKED AND INSEPARABLE DESTINIES · Fe

FORMULA I: INTERLINKED AND INSEPARABLE DESTINIES · Ferrari and

I: INTERLINKED AND INSEPARABLE DESTINIES · Ferrari and Formula I:

LINKED AND INSEPARABLE DESTINIES · Ferrari and Formula 1: interlin

AND INSEPARABLE DESTINIES · Ferrari and Formula 1: interlinked and i

nterlinked and insepara

ed and inseparable dest

Ferrari and Formula 1: interlinked and inseparable destinies

nseparable destinies FE

le destinies FERRARI A

and Formula 1: interlinked and inseparable destinies FERRARI AND FOR

mula 1: interlinked and inseparable destinies FERRARI AND FORMULA

interlinked and inseparable destinies FERRARI AND FORMULA I: INT

linked and inseparable destinies FERRARI AND FORMULA I: INTERLINK

inseparable destinies FERRARI AND FORMULA I: INTERLINKED AND II

ble destinies FERRARI AND FORMULA I: INTERLINKED AND INSEPAR

tinies · FERRARI AND FORMULA I: INTERLINKED AND INSEPARABLE

ES • Ferrari and Formula 1: interlinked and inseparable destinies •FERRA-

rari and Formula 1: interlinked and inseparable destinies FERRARI AND

ormula 1: interlinked and inseparable destinies FERRARI AND FORMULA

nterlinked and inseparable destinies FERRARI AND FORMULA 1: INTER-

ed and inseparable destinies FERRARI AND FORMULA 1: INTERLINKED

separable destinies FERRARI AND FORMULA 1: INTERLINKED AND IN-

le destinies FERRARI AND FORMULA 1: INTERLINKED AND INSEPARA-

ies FERRARI AND FORMULA 1: INTERLINKED AND INSEPARABLE DES-

RARI AND FORMULA 1: INTERLINKED AND INSEPARABLE DESTINIES •

D FORMULA 1: INTERLINKED AND INSEPARABLE DESTINIES • Ferrari

MULA 1: INTERLINKED AND INSEPARABLE DESTINIES • Ferrari and For-

: INTERLINKED AND INSEPARABLE DESTINIES • Ferrari and Formula 1:

RLINKED AND INSEPARABLE DESTINIES • Ferrari and Formula 1: inter-

D AND INSEPARABLE DESTINIES • Ferrari and Formula 1: interlinked and

SEPARABLE DESTINIES • Ferrari and Formula 1: interlinked and insepara-

LE DESTINIES • Ferrari and Formula 1: interlinked and inseparable des-

STINIES • Ferrari and Formula 1: interlinked and inseparable destinies •

The history of Ferrari is scattered with fantastic on-road vehicles; but it all began on the racetrack, and that tie is and will always be indestructible.

There are practically no championships or prestigious races that have not seen the Prancing Horse on the starting line: Formula One, Formula Two, FIA European Hill Climb, World Sportscar Championship, Le Mans, Daytona, Sebring, Mille Miglia, Targa Florio, Giro di Sicilia, IMSA, Carrera Panamericana.

Many other carmakers, although they can boast considerable sporting success, have had fluctuating relations with these races. Some have raced for long periods, followed by long pauses during which they withdrew to enjoy the return on image from the races, or to lick their wounds; but not Ferrari.

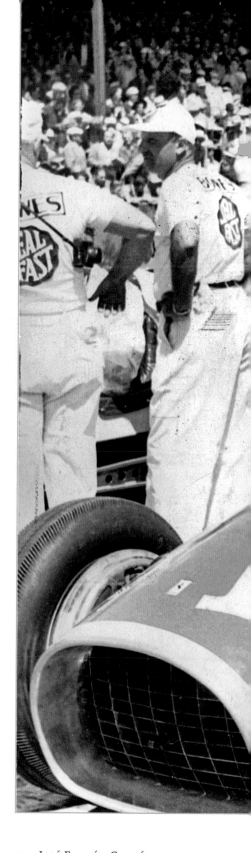

Although there have been some frustrating periods without wins, the *Scuderia* has always been present in competitions since the nineteen-thirties—when it was not yet an independent car manufacturer, but only a racing branch of Alfa Romeo.

Until the seventies, the company competed in a wide range of competitions, until the Drake, as Enzo Ferrari was known, decided to concentrate all efforts on Formula One—which had become extremely expensive, but left the possibility for individuals to race with the "reds" or for some trusted partners to use engines "made in Maranello."

There were also numerous successes in those races: for example, the rallies between 1974 and 1977 with the Lancia Stratos running the Dino Ferrari engine; the victory of the Ferrari 333 SP in the

30 • JOSÉ FROILÁN GONZÁLEZ (SECOND FROM LEFT) RECEIVING CONGRATULATIONS AFTER WINNING THE 1951 BRITISH GRAND PRIX: IT WAS THE FIRST FERRARI F1 VICTORY.

30–31 • ALBERTO ASCARI DRIVING THE CAR IN WHICH HE UNSUCCESSFULLY COMPETED IN THE 1952 INDIANAPOLIS 500. HOWEVER, IN THE SAME YEAR HE BECAME F1 WORLD CHAMPION.

American IMSA 1995 championship; or the many wins in the international FIA GT, between 2005 and 2009, of the Maserati MC12, clone of the Ferrari Enzo. But the principal source of glory—and of the most burning disappointments—has been Formula One.

Ferrari made its debut in the first world championship in history, in 1950, but only participated in the second Gran Prix (GP) in Monte Carlo, where it took second place with Alberto Ascari at the wheel. In the Italian GP, Dorino Serafini was the driver who gained second place for the team.

However, 1951 saw the first victory in the United Kingdom, thanks to the Argentinian driver José Froilán González. Others followed. The Prancing Horse won its first Formula One qualification thanks to five consecutive victories by Ascari and one by Piero Taruffi.

Ascari won again in 1953, standing five more times on the podium, while Mike Hawthorn and Giuseppe Farina won one GP each.

In 1954 and 1955, Ferrari faced a very strong Mercedes team, and in the first two years they only had two successes with González and Hawthorn and, the following year, one with Maurice Trintignant.

In 1955, Lancia withdrew from competition following the death of Ascari and handed all the material from the racing teams to the Prancing Horse, including the D50 single-seater. It was in this car that the Argentinian Juan Manuel Fangio won the championship in 1956, winning in Argentina, United Kingdom, and Germany, while the British driver Peter Collins won first place in Belgium and in France.

1957 was a quiet year for Ferrari, marked by the tragic death of Eugenio Castellotti during a test drive in Modena. In 1958, they won another title with Hawthorn, who won just once, in the French GP. The year was not without tragedy for the Modena-based company: Peter Collins and Luigi Musso were both involved in fatal accidents.

The next two editions of the championship were dominated by the Cooper cars, and Ferrari had to be content with two victories, by Tony Brooks in 1959 and Phil Hill in 1960.

Ferrari's first Formula One World Constructors' Championship (WCC, introduced in 1958) came in 1961, thanks to Phil Hill—who was also world champion with two victories—and to Wolfgang von Trips, who also won two GPs before dying in an accident during a race at Monza.

At the end of the season, following a palace revolution described elsewhere in this book, the technical top management was ousted and the team suffered a brief period of confusion. In 1962 there were no victories, while the following year only the British driver John Surtees won in Germany.

However, by 1964, the Prancing Horse brought home the World Drivers' Championship (WDC) with Surtees, with two personal successes, and also the WCC, thanks to the success of Lorenzo Bandini in Austria.

However, this was the start of a lean decade, at least in terms of absolute titles, although Surtees and Ludovico Scarfiotti both won in 1966 and the Belgian Jacky Ickx won in 1968.

32 TOP • JUAN MANUEL FANGIO DURING THE 1956 GERMAN GP TRIALS.

32 BOTTOM • PETER COLLINS (LEFT) AND MIKE HAWTHORN AT THE 1958 BRITISH GP.

33 • THE START OF THE 1955 MONTE CARLO GP: ALBERTO ASCARI, IN HIS LANCIA D50 N.26, SPRINTING BETWEEN JUAN MANUEL FANGIO'S AND STIRLING MOSS'S MERCEDES CARS.

The situation improved in 1970 thanks to three wins by Ickx and one, in Italy, by the Swiss driver Clay Regazzoni. That year, the Belgian came second in the final ranking, behind the Austrian driver Jochen Rindt, who was given the title posthumously because he died in the qualifying races for the GP in Monza.

The following year, the American Mario Andretti and Ickx each brought home a victory, and Ickx won again in 1972.

1973 was a dark year for Ferrari. For the first time in its history in Formula One, it did not even reach the podium. But the situation began to turn around in 1974 with the victories of the Austrian Niki Lauda in Spain and Holland and of Regazzoni in Germany.

This was merely the prelude to the triumphs of the following year: Lauda won the WDC thanks to five victories, and even the WCC did not escape them, thanks to the contribution of Regazzoni in Italy.

34 • JACKY ICKX, IN HIS FERRARI 312 IN MONZA, 1968, WAS A WHISKER FROM THE F1 CHAMPIONSHIP IN 1970, BUT THE TITLE WAS GIVEN POSTHUMOUSLY TO JOCHEN RINDT.

35 • CLAY REGAZZONI, HERE AT THE 1974 AUSTRIAN GP DRIVING A FERRARI 312 B3, WAS ONE OF THE BEST-LOVED DRIVERS OF ALL TIME AT MARANELLO, EVEN THOUGH HE NEVER WON THE F1 CHAMPIONSHIP.

In 1976, the WCC came again thanks to a further five wins by Lauda and one by Regazzoni. Lauda lost the WDC by a whisker due to his appalling accident at the Nürburgring.

Another brace of world championships followed in 1977: Lauda became world champion thanks to three wins, and the Argentinian Carlos Reutemann contributed to the WCC.

Reutemann had four wins in 1978, while the Canadian Gilles Villeneuve took first place in the Canadian GP.

Nothing suggested that a new and lengthy lean period was about to start when, in 1979, the South African Jody Scheckter made his debut in Ferrari, winning three races and the Drivers' Championship, and also thanks to Villeneuve's three wins, leading the Scuderia Fer-

rari to the WCC. In contrast, 1980 was another nightmare year, because the new single-seater, despite the fact that it was based on the winning car from the previous year, never did better than fifth place.

Things went better in 1982, with two epic successes by Villeneuve in Monte Carlo and Spain, but in 1982 the Canadian driver, considered almost a son by the Drake, was killed during a qualifying race in Belgium. Misfortune had not abandoned the team, because the French driver Didier Pironi, teammate of Villeneuve, after two wins was involved in a terrifying accident in Germany, which ended his career as a driver. The Drivers' Championship eluded them, but not the WCC, also thanks to the victory in Germany of the French driver Patrick Tambay, who joined the team to replace Villeneuve.

36–37 • After a long barren period, Niki Lauda, seen here in his 312T at the 1975 Belgian GP, won Ferrari the longed-for drivers' title in the same year.

37 • An intense portrait of Canadian driver Gilles Villeneuve, who died prematurely in 1982: Ferrari fans took him to their hearts more than any other driver, because of his daring driving.

The WCC went to Ferrari in 1983, thanks to the three successes of the French driver René Arnoux, and Tambay's one.

The great news of 1984 was the arrival in the team of an Italian, Michele Alboreto, eleven years after the departure of Arturo Merzario.

Alboreto began by winning well in Belgium, and even grazed the title in 1985 thanks to victories in Canada and Germany.

Unfortunately, in 1986 there were no wins for Ferrari, while in 1987 and 1988 (the year Enzo Ferrari died) the only three victories went to the Austrian Gerhard Berger.

The championship also got away in 1989, despite the two wins by the British driver Nigel Mansell and one by Berger. However, we can consider as a sort of moral victory for Ferrari the introduction of the semi-automatic transmission controlled by the driver using two paddles, which revolutionized the world of Formula One.

In 1990, the fast-moving Frenchman Alain Proust came to Ferrari, winning five GPs, while Mansell won a sixth. Still, none of this was enough to win either of the titles. The following three years were even worse: no Prancing Horse came in first place.

It was not until 1994 that Berger won in Germany, a victory repeated the following year by the Frenchman Jean Alesi in Canada.

The car readied for 1996 was not one of the fastest, but Ferrari could count on the advent of the German driver Michael Schumacher, who won three victories, inaugurating his legendary era.

In 1997, the German won five times, and six times in 1998; and the Ferrari team finally won the WCC again in 1999. It did not win the WDC because Schumacher, who had scored two victories, broke his leg during the British GP. However, his teammate, the British driver Eddie Irvine, was a contender for the Drivers' Championship, having won four GPs.

38–39 • THE WINNERS OF THE MEXICAN GP IN 1990: FIRST NIGEL MANSELL, SECOND ALAIN PROST, BOTH IN FERRARIS. GERHARD BERGER CAME THIRD IN A McLAREN. THE AUSTRIAN IN HIS TURN DROVE A FERRARI IN 1987, AND RETURNED TO IT IN 1993.

39 • THE FRENCHMAN JEAN ALESI: ANOTHER SPECTACULAR DRIVER WHO MADE FERRARI FANS DREAM, EVEN THOUGH IN THE END HE CLAIMED ONLY ONE VICTORY FOR FERRARI, IN 1995.

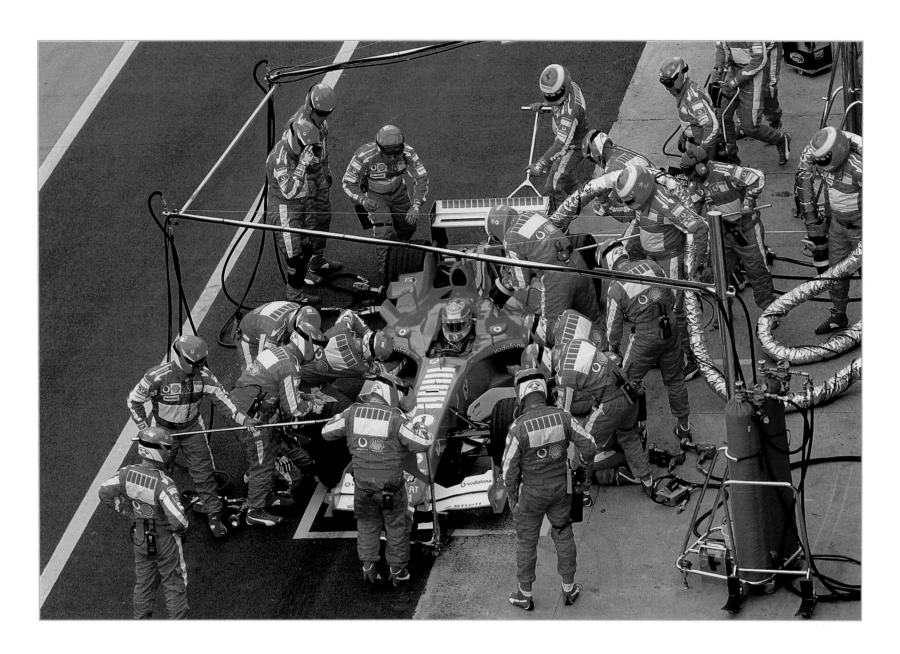

And so we come to our days. After 21 years of absence, in 2000 Schumacher dominated the championship, winning nine GPs, to which we must add the victory of the Brazilian driver Rubens Barrichello. Both titles went to Maranello.

The same thing happened in 2001, when the German driver chalked up no fewer than eleven victories. At this point, Formula One had become almost monothematic.

In 2002, Ferrari left only two GPs out of seventeen to their competitors: thanks to a further eleven for Schumacher and four for Barrichello, the WCC and the WDC did not go to others, as in the next two years.

In 2003, there were six wins for Schumacher and two for Barrichello. In 2004, Schumacher totaled thirteen successes, to which we must add two for Barrichello.

At this point, Ferrari's supremacy suddenly ended. In 2005, Schumacher won only one GP, in the United States. The following year, the situation improved, with seven victories for Schumacher and two for the Brazilian Felipe Massa, but this was not enough to win the championships.

In 2007, another glorious year, Kimi Räikkönen won the championship in his first year at Maranello with six victories. Three wins by Massa brought home the WCC.

40 • MICHAEL SCHUMACHER WAS THE HERO OF AN EPIC—AND PERHAPS UNREPEATABLE—ERA: FROM 1999 TO 2004, HE WON FERRARI 5 WORLD DRIVERS' TITLES AND 6 CONSTRUCTORS' TITLES.

41• MICHAEL SCHUMACHER'S FERRARI SURROUNDED BY MECHANICS DURING A PIT STOP IN THE 2005 CANADIAN GP, WHICH TOOK PLACE ON THE MONTREAL CIRCUIT.

2008 did not go too badly, with the WCC won thanks to two victories by Räikkönen and six by Massa—who, however, lost the WDC by a whisker in the last race.

Then another lean period began. In 2009, during the qualifying races for the Grand Prix in Hungary, Massa was knocked unconscious by a spring that had become detached from Barrichello's car, and he missed the last eight GPs of the season, while Räikkönen only won in Belgium.

The long-awaited arrival of Fernando Alonso in 2010 improved the situation, but did not bring any championships, even though the Spaniard won five times in 2010, once in 2011, three times in 2012, and twice in 2013. In 2014, things got even worse, because neither Alonso nor Räikkönen managed to take a first place. At this point, Sebastian Vettel joined the team, but the German driver did not bring the desired results, even though he won three times in 2015 and five times in 2017 and again in 2018.

The 2019 season does not reverse the performance of the team, which manages to place only three wins in total, two of the new entry from Monte Carlo, Charles Leclerc, in Belgium and Italy, and one of Vettel in Singapore.

42 • 2012 European GP at Valencia: Fernando Alonso, at the top on the right, won in front of Kimi Räikkönen and Michael Schumacher. However, the Spanish driver would not succeed in winning titles for Ferrari.

42–43 • Sebastian Vettel celebrates his victory in the Singapore GP of 2019. The German came to Maranello in 2015, already having won four Formula 1 championships with Red Bull from 2010 to 2013.

The sports history of Ferrari is destined to continue, enhanced by a record of achievements that so far, even considering only the most important competitions, includes fifteen Formula One World Drivers' Championships and sixteen World Constructors' Championships; the team has won thirteen World Sportscar Championships, fourteen editions of the 12 Hours of Sebring, nine of the 24 Heures du Mans, eight of the Mille Miglia, seven of the Targa Florio, five of the 24 Hours of Daytona, and two of the Carrera Panamericana.

44–45 • CHARLES LECLERC CROSSES THE FINISHING LINE OF THE RUSSIAN GP IN THIRD POSITION. RIGHT FROM HIS FIRST YEAR, THE MONEGASQUE DRIVER HAS SHOWED THAT HE IS FERRARI'S HOPE FOR THE FUTURE.

45 • SEBASTIAN VETTEL (LEFT) AND CHARLES LECLERC (RIGHT) ARE THE TWO 2019 FORMULA 1 DRIVERS FOR FERRARI: FROM THE START, A DIFFICULT RELATIONSHIP EXISTED BETWEEN THESE TWO VERY FAST DRIVERS, BOTH DEMONSTRATING STRONG CHARACTERS.

Before all else, a “factory” made of people

• Before all else, a “factory” made of people • Before all else,
people • Before all else, a “factory” made of people • Before all els
people • Before all else, a “factory” made of people • Before all
of people • Before all else, a “factory” made of people • Before all e
people • Before all else, a “factory” made of people • Before all
of people • Before all else, a “factory” made of people • Before all e
tory” made of people • Before all
ory” made of people • Before all e
tory” made of people • Before all
of people • Before all else, a “factory” made of people • Before all e
people • Before all else, a “factory” made of people • Before all
of people • Before all else, a “factory” made of people • Before all e
people • Before all else, a “factory” made of people • Before all
of people • Before all else, a “factory” made of people • Before all e
people • Before all else, a “factory” made of people • Before all e
people • Before all else, a “factory” made of people • Before all else, a

actory" made of people • BEFORE ALL ELSE, A "FACTORY" MADE OF

A "FACTORY" MADE OF PEOPLE • Before all else, a "factory" made of

e, a "factory" made of people • BEFORE ALL ELSE, A "FACTORY" MADE

A "FACTORY" MADE OF PEOPLE • Before all else, a "factory" made of

e, a "factory" made of people • BEFORE ALL ELSE, A "FACTORY" MADE

A "FACTORY" MADE OF PEOPLE • Before all else, a "factory" made of

e, a "factory" made of people • BEFORE ALL ELSE, A "FACTORY" MADE

A "FACTORY" MADE OF PEOPLE • Before all else, a "factory" made of

e, a "factory" made of people • BEFORE ALL ELSE, A "FACTORY" MADE

A "FACTORY" MADE OF PEOPLE • Before all else, a "factory" made of

e, a "factory" made of people • BEFORE ALL ELSE, A "FACTORY" MADE

A "FACTORY" MADE OF PEOPLE • Before all else, a "factory" made of

e, a "factory" made of people • BEFORE ALL ELSE, A "FACTORY" MADE

A "FACTORY" MADE OF PEOPLE • Before all else, a "factory" made of

e, a "factory" made of people • BEFORE ALL ELSE, A "FACTORY" MADE

A "FACTORY" MADE OF PEOPLE • Before all else, a "factory" made of

a "factory" made of people • BEFORE ALL ELSE, A "FACTORY" MADE OF

ACTORY" MADE OF PEOPLE • Before all else, a "factory" made of people •

When Enzo Ferrari set up his company in 1947, after having managed the sporting activities of Alfa Romeo, he had no experience as a constructor. However, he had an important insight. "I believe," he loved to say, "that factories are made up of cars, buildings, and people. Ferrari is above all made up of people."

He was not even an engineer—he received his degree *honoris causa* from the University of Bologna only in 1960 for his obvious industrial and sporting success—but he described himself as an "inspirer of men." And of spirits. He pushed his people to the limit, and so he obtained the best. Or else he let them go when they did not fully match his requirements and ideas.

He would not hear of compromise when the good of Ferrari was at stake, and so close relationships with him were not easy.

"I have found," he related, "men who undoubtedly loved the automobile as much as I do. But perhaps I have found no others with the same stubbornness, driven by this same governing passion in life, which in my case has taken away the time and the taste for almost anything else. I have no other interest apart from the racing car."

Therefore, we must not be surprised that—apart from that of its founder—the history of the Maranello is studded with highly significant personalities, no less than with wonderful and often winning cars. These people have had a leading role in crucial moments, mostly marvelous, but some in dramatic or breaking moments.

For example, at the end of October 1961 the Drake was still suffering from the loss of his son Dino when the so-called "palace revolution" took place. Mystery still surrounds the events leading up to the dismissal with immediate effect of as many as eight key figures in the Maranello Scuderia. According to some rumors, Enzo Ferrari's wife, Laura Garello, who took an active part in the company life, slapped one of the eight on the racetrack because of a difference of opinion, and a formal request was made by the group involved that she be banned from the tracks. The result was the "Grand Old Man's" reaction: he unhesitatingly dismissed all the signatories. In fact, in doing so one could say that he shot himself in the foot by decapitating the Ferrari top management, creating quite a few problems for the company. Among those dismissed, just to give a few names: the designer Carlo Chiti, the manager of prototype testing Giotto Bizzarrini, and the sporting director Romolo Tavoni. There were also personalities who did not stay long at Maranello but made their mark, because they contributed new ideas, successes, or simply emotions: for example, Gilles Villeneuve.

The Canadian driver won only six Grands Prix—nothing compared with the results obtained by Lauda or Schumacher—and never won a world title, but made Ferrari supporters dream because of his courage, speed, and sincerity. Also, Enzo Ferrari was fond of him and thought of him almost as a son. Although he was at Maranello for comparatively little time and died in a dramatic accident in 1982, Gilles contributed enormously to the image of the Prancing Horse and today is still in the hearts of fans more than other drivers with many titles.

Also Michele Alboreto did no better than runner-up to the world champion, but actually sacrificed his career for Ferrari, passing up the call from a winning Williams team to stay at Maranello. He was an Italian, and it was too long since there had been an Italian driver at Ferrari. Perhaps he felt his presence in the red car as a mission; and the Drake was also fond of him for this reason.

However, there was never any love lost between Enzo Ferrari and some other great names who passed through Modena: Alberto Ascari and Juan Manuel Fangio won world titles with Ferrari, which were important "items" in his list of victories, but the first was too "combative" for the great boss, the second too reserved and wary.

And probably not even the cold, calculating Niki Lauda completely won the heart of Ferrari; but in the nineteen-seventies, Ferrari needed him and he took Ferrari to the top of the world.

On the other hand, it was perhaps the Tuscan instinctiveness and restlessness of the already-mentioned Giotto Bizzarrini and Carlo Chiti, but also of Aurelio Lampredi, which got in the way of a lasting relationship with the Drake; but they were first-rate designers, useful for the cause and their time in Maranello brought important results. Below we give profiles of the figures mentioned here briefly and of others who have made the Prancing Horse great, above all Michael Schumacher, to remember and relive their unforgettable stories at Maranello.

AURELIO LAMPREDI
(engineer)

After receiving his diploma from the Technical College of Fribourg, in Switzerland, Aurelio Lampredi began his working life as a designer at the Cantieri Navali (shipyards) in Livorno. He then moved to Piaggio, to the Fonderie Bassoli and to the Officine Meccaniche Reggiane-Caproni. Here he attracted attention as an engine designer and was recommended to Enzo Ferrari, who appointed him in September 1946. The first period at Maranello, however, only lasted until 1947 because of disagreements with Giuseppe Busso and Gioacchino Colombo. Thus he moved to Isotta Fraschini, telling the Drake he would be willing to return when he could work independently; he did just that a few months later.

At Maranello, he dedicated himself to developing the V12, which, when mounted on Froilan Gonzalez's 375, gained Ferrari its first success in Formula 1. Then he designed the 500 F2 4-cylinder engine, which won Ferrari championships in 1952 and 1953 with Alberto Ascari.

However, in 1955, he clashed with Enzo Ferrari because of his project for an unusual two-cylinder engine for Formula 1, which would never be achieved; and so he moved to Fiat.

In the beginning at Fiat, he worked on an overhead straight six-cylinder valve engine for the 1800 and 2100, which appeared in 1959, and then on the four-cylinder engines of the 1300 and the 1500 in 1961. He later designed the engine of the 124 which, updated in various ways, was used from 1966 to 2000, and also adapted the V6 of the Ferrari Dino for use on the Fiat Dino coupé and roadster.

In 1977, he perfected the four-cylinder 1050 engine to be produced in the Fiat plant in Belo Horizonte, Brazil; it was also used on the Fiat 127 second series and on the Ritmo, for which he also designed a diesel engine. He stayed at Fiat until 1982, when he retired.

50 • AURELIO LAMPREDI (CENTER), NEAR NINO FARINA'S FERRARI SHORTLY BEFORE THE START OF THE 1954 BELGIAN GP. UNFORTUNATELY, THE CAR WOULD NOT FINISH THE RACE BECAUSE OF AN IGNITION PROBLEM.

GIUSEPPE BUSSO
(designer)

Giuseppe Busso worked at Maranello from 1946 until nearly the end of 1947. Thus, we can say that he was present at the Ferrari's first steps. He had joined Fiat in 1937 as a designer in the airplane engine department, and then moved in 1938 to the experimental railroad vehicle department. In 1939 he changed to Alfa Romeo to work on special studies for racing cars. Here he met Gioachino Colombo.

The latter, suspended by Alfa in 1945 because he was accused of collaboration during the war, became a technical consultant for Ferrari and suggested Busso as director of the technical office, which was already developing the 125 S.

Busso accepted and took on two other projects, which, however, would never become reality: a 1500 cc 12-cylinder single-seater with a supercharger, and a sportscar with a 6-cylinder engine made by splitting the 125 S engine in two. He also studied a revolutionary type of rear suspension, and worked on the project and construction of the two-liter Tipo 159 which would win the Gran Premio Città di Torino, driven by Raymond Sommer, in 1947. But in the fall of 1946, Aurelio Lampredi arrived at Maranello, in the role of Busso and Colombo's associate. At this point, differences of opinion arose, and the flying of sparks between the three great designers with strong personalities was inevitable.

Thus Busso returned to Milan at the end of 1947, like many other technicians who had come to Maranello from Alfa Romeo, after also having collaborated on project 166. He came back to Alfa in 1948, where, by a twist of fate, in 1951 he again found Gioachino Colombo, who had also returned from Ferrari. Here he designed the V6 engine, unanimously recognized as one of the best Alfa engines in history. He left active service in 1977 in the position of co-central director.

Enzo Ferrari described Giuseppe Busso as "a capable and stubborn technician."

52 • The "dream team" of Alfa technicians at the beginning of the nineteen-sixties: left to right, Orazio Satta Puliga, Giuseppe Busso, Giuseppe Luraghi, and Carlo Chiti. Busso and Chiti had already had a brilliant history at Maranello.

ALBERTO ASCARI
(driver)

The son of Antonio Ascari, one of the greats of motorsport, Alberto started on motorcycles in 1936 and four years later changed to cars, taking part in the Mille Miglia in an Auto Avio Costruzioni 815, the first auto built by Enzo Ferrari when he could not yet use his own name in his car-making business. After the Second World War, Luigi Villoresi, another great Italian driver, and also partner and friend, urged Ascari to go back to racing. He started again with Maserati and Alfa Romeo, but in 1949 he entered the Ferrari orbit. He made his debut in Formula 1 with a second place in the 1950 Monaco GP behind Juan Manuel Fangio.

In 1952, he dominated the championship, winning six GPs and winning the first title for Ferrari, and he did the same thing again in 1953, this time winning five races. In the meantime, Lancia also had decided to take part in Formula 1 and offered Ascari rewards that the new world champion could hardly refuse. Indeed, he took Gigi Villoresi, his deputy at Maranello, with him.

But the development of the car, christened D50, was difficult and Ascari only managed to take part in the last GP of 1954. 1955 could have been a better year, but it began in the worst way possible, because in

the second GP at Monte Carlo Ascari drove into the sea, remaining unhurt. However, four days later, he went to Monza on a courtesy visit to Eugenio Castellotti, who was putting the final touches to a Ferrari 750. Ascari asked him if he could try the car, but he crashed and lost his life at the curve that still bears his name. The accident has never been completely explained. Lancia, which was in financial difficulties, took the opportunity to announce its withdrawal from competition and handed over all its material to the Scuderia Ferrari, which in 1956 won the World Championship with a car derived precisely from the D50.

As of today, Alberto Ascari is the last Italian driver to win the Formula 1 Championship.

54 • ALBERTO ASCARI AT THE BRITISH GP, WHICH HE WON IN 1953. THE MILANESE DRIVER WON TITLES IN 1952 AND 1953 FOR FERRARI AND IS THE LAST ITALIAN TO BECOME FORMULA 1 CHAMPION.

55 • A VERY YOUNG ASCARI IN TESTS. HE CAME TO FERRARI IN 1949, BUT NEVER CAME TO A TOTAL UNDERSTANDING WITH ENZO FERRARI, DESPITE MANY SUCCESSES.

SERGIO SCAGLIETTI
(entrepreneur)

Sergio Scaglietti had a passion for constructing cars from childhood: at eight years old, he already enjoyed building rudimentary racing cars. In 1933, although he was only thirteen, he began to work in a motor body shop and became the panel beater for repairing racing car fenders. In 1939, he met Enzo Ferrari, with whom he created a very solid professional relationship, which in time was to turn into friendship. The Drake, who in those years was managing the Scuderia Ferrari, responsible for Alfa Romeo sporting activities, happened to be in the workshop where Scaglietti was working and noticed the quality of his work on an Alfa that, apart from anything else, improved the original lines of the car. From that moment on, he advised drivers and customers needing repairs to go to the young "panel beater."

In 1951 Scaglietti opened his body works, and the Drake—who in the meantime had founded Ferrari—began to commission bodies for his cars from him. The first commission was to build the shells for the 500 Mondial, and from then on the activities of the *carrozzeria* Scaglietti were completely absorbed by Ferrari. Working in close contact with Pininfarina, Scaglietti originated some of the most famous Ferraris of the 1950s, 1960s, and 1970s: 250 Testa Rossa, 250 GT California, 250 GTO, and Dino 206/246; he also contributed to the 365 Daytona.

In 1959, Scaglietti called on his sons Oscar and Claudio to work in the company, and he continued to collaborate with Ferrari as an external supplier—which, however, in 1975 incorporated it by buying a majority shareholding. In 1997 Ferrari decided to use the name Scaglietti for the official car personalization program and, in 2003, it also used the name for the coupé 2+2 612, the heir of the 400/412s.

57 • SERGIO SCAGLIETTI WAS A GREAT FRIEND OF ENZO FERRARI'S, AS WELL AS BEING THE CREATOR OF THE "ROSSE," THE ICONIC RED CAR BODIES, UNTIL THE MID-SEVENTIES, WHEN HIS COMPANY WAS TAKEN OVER BY FERRARI.

LUIGI CHINETTI
(mechanic, driver, entrepreneur)

Luigi Chinetti, almost a contemporary of Enzo Ferrari's, began working at the age of 14 in his father's workshop. He then joined Alfa Romeo as a mechanic in the experiment section. In 1925, he moved to France to assist Antonio Ascari in the Montihéry race and stayed there to look after the Alfa Romeos sold to the Conte di Carrobio. In 1925 he also began his career as a driver, culminating in his 1932 victory at the Le Mans 24-Hour race in the Alfa 8C with Raymond Sommer. Among others, they beat the official Alfa Romeo team.

He became an American national and in 1949 turned up at Maranello to purchase a 166 MM. Here he met Enzo Ferrari, with whom he shared interests and opinions on motor racing. In that same year he again won at Le Mans, only giving up the wheel to his co-driver for an hour, and then the 24 Hours at Spa, gaining for Ferrari a considerable international fame.

In 1954, Enzo Ferrari appointed him agent for North America, opening up a market which was to become a priority for the Ferrari road cars.

In 1958, Chinetti created the North American Racing Team, the American extension of the Scuderia Ferrari, with which he won the first of many races in 1962: the Paris 1000 km at Monthléry, thanks to the Ferrari 250 GTO driven by Ricardo and Pedro Rodriguez. Until it ceased operations in 1982, the North American Racing Team took part in more than 200 races and employed more than 100 drivers, among them Stirling Moss, Phil Hill, Giancarlo Baghetti, Umberto Maglioli, Nino Vaccarella, and Mario Andretti.

In the meantime, the relationship with the Drake had also turned into a friendship, so much so that in 1975, when Ferrari decided to export its cars on its own, the Commendatore, atypically, ordered that Chinetti receive a percentage on every car sold.

58 • The Ferrari 340 MM of Chinetti and Tom Cole in the 1953 Le Mans 24-Hour Race. Unfortunately, Cole was killed in a terrible accident.

59 • An intense expression is on the face of the Italo-American Luigi Chinetti while he follows "his" Ferraris in the 1964 edition of the famous Le Mans 24-Hour Race.

JUAN MANUEL FANGIO
(driver)

60–61 • Enzo Ferrari and Juan Manuel Fangio at the 1956 Italian GP: their relationship was often marked by conflict,
as always happens with two dominant personalities.

Fangio began his career in his native land, where his courage and physical strength enabled him to win races on difficult tracks. But he also demonstrated a precise style of driving and considerable mechanical knowledge. He drove in his first European race in 1948, but only in the following year did he begin to race and win regularly there. Enzo Ferrari was fascinated by his speed and intelligence, and so Fangio arrived at Maranello in 1956, when his achievements already included three Formula 1 Championships, won in 1951 with Alfa Romeo and in 1954 and 1955 with Daimler-Benz.

But Fangio seemed to the Drake to be so shy and wary that placing him on the team was a difficult prospect. The season started in July, with the GP of Argentina, and Fangio won immediately. Then in July he again finished first in Britain; this was repeated in August in Germany. Enzo Ferrari's investment thus gave excellent results, because with his three victories and two second places at Monte Carlo and in Italy, the Argentinian won the drivers' title in front of Stirling Moss and his teammate Peter Collins.

But the relationship between Fangio (who proved to be too individualistic), the Scuderia, and Enzo Ferrari did not work either on the track or off it, and at the end of the season the Argentinian said good-bye to the Prancing Horse.

But this was not the end of his successes, because the next year he raced with Maserati and won his last world title. Then, in 1958, he took part in the occasional race and at the end of the season retired from competition to become an entrepreneur.

His record of five world titles would be matched only in 2002 by Michael Schumacher, with none other than Ferrari. (The German, however, would win two more, setting the present record.)

61 • Fangio in the German GP of 1956, in which he won both the pole position and victory. In that year, he also achieved the Formula 1 title for Ferrari: it was his third personal title.

GIOTTO BIZZARRINI
(designer)

Bizzarrini was the real father of the 250 GTO (1962), which is still the most valued Ferrari for collectors. This gives him a place on the Olympus of designers, and on the list of men who have made the Prancing Horse great. Bizzarrini graduated in Engineering from the University of Pisa in 1953 and in the following year was hired by Alfa Romeo as a test engineer. In 1957, the test engineer Sergio Sighinolfi died in an accident, and the Drake asked his technical director Andrea Fraschetti to suggest a good replacement. Thus, Bizzarrini met Enzo Ferrari and was appointed on February 6, with the task of assisting Luigi Bazzi in the test department. One of Bizzarrini's first achievements was the introduction of a new type of self-ventilating disc brake. In August the same year, during tests at the Aerautodromo di Modena, Andrea Fraschetti also died. At this point, Bizzarrini had to recommend a qualified technician, and Giotto suggested his fellow Tuscan Carlo Chiti, who was known and appreciated from the Alfa days. Thus, the pair was formed who built some of the most beautiful and effective automobiles in history.

The first car designed by Bizzarrini at Maranello was the 250 Testa Rossa, after which Enzo Ferrari promoted him to the production control and testing department. The first project for the 250 GTO was his, but in 1961 Bizzarrini and Chiti were dismissed together with six other associates following the "palace revolution." Thus opened the era of Mauro Forghieri, who would then finish the development of the GTO.

Bizzarrini thus moved to ATS, of which Chiti himself was among the founders. Then he moved on to the Scuderia Serenissima of Conte Volpi di Misurata and collaborated with Lamborghini and Iso Rivolta. In 1964, he founded his Prototipi Bizzarrini and designed another legendary model: the 5300 GT Strada.

62–63 • ONE OF THE FIRST TESTS ON THE LEGENDARY FERRARI 250 GTO AT MONZA IN 1961. IN THE BACKGROUND, GIOTTO BIZZARRINI GIVES INSTRUCTIONS TO THE BELGIAN DRIVER WILLY MAIRESSE, WHO IS TESTING THE PROTOTYPE.

CARLO CHITI
(engineer)

Carlo Chiti, who was an engineer with an aeronautics background, gained his first experience in Alfa Romeo, where in 1952 he was assigned to the racing and special experiment section. In 1957 he was called up by Enzo Ferrari, through the intervention of Giotto Bizzarrini.

It was also thanks to Chiti that Ferrari agreed to modify one of his fundamental theories, that the engine must necessarily be front-mounted. It was a good choice, because in 1961 Chiti's 156 F1 won the Drivers' World Championship and, for the first time, won the Constructors' Championship for Ferrari.

Besides those two titles, the cars designed by Carlo Chiti also won the 1958 Formula 1 World Championship with Mike Hawthorn, and three World Sportscar Championships in 1958, 1960, and 1961.

Also in 1961, however, he left Ferrari with seven other technicians and managers because of internal conflicts with Enzo Ferrari's wife, which culminated in the so-called "palace revolution," and moved to ATS, which he also co-founded and managed in the beginning. He remained there until 1964.

He then moved to Autodelta, a company preparing Alfa Romeo racing cars, and in 1966 became the CEO and director.

For the next twenty years, he was responsible for Alfa Romeo sporting activity, contributing to winning two World Sportscar Championships, in 1975 and 1977, and bringing it back into Formula 1 in 1976, first as an engine supplier to Brabham, then with a one-seater completely built by Alfa. This attempt, however, was unsuccessful despite its great promise.

In 1985, he founded Motori Moderni, a company established with the aim of designing and building racing cars; it mainly supplied Scuderia Minardi.

64–65 • CARLO CHITI AND ENZO FERRARI, LEFT AND SECOND FROM LEFT, AT THE COMMISSIONING OF THE 156 REAR-ENGINED ONE-SEATER WHICH WOULD WIN WITH THE AMERICAN PHIL HILL IN 1961.

GIAMPAOLO DALLARA
(engineer)

In 1959, after graduating from the faculty of aeronautical engineering of the Politecnico di Milano, Giampaolo Dallara arrived at the Ferrari racing department as Carlo Chiti's assistant. But after only two years of Formula 1, prototypes and granturismo moved to the racing department of Maserati.

In any case, they were two intense and extremely instructive years for Dallara, who described the Ferrari Scuderia as "a continuous university." In any event, he made an excellent impression on the Drake, who in the next few years tried to bring him to Maranello, but without success.

However, from then on Dallara kept up his relationship with Ferrari, which motorized many of his designs for Formula 1. But in addition to this, from 1963 to 1969 Dallara worked at Lamborghini, where he directed a group of technicians designing the Miura. The next stage was De Tomaso, where he also designed the 1970 Formula 1 single-seater. In 1972, he founded his Dallara Automobili da Competizione, with which he designed some prototypes and also collaborated with Alfa Romeo Corse. In 1973 his relationship with Iso began, both for building the Formula 1 single-seater and for the production of road sportscars.

From 1974 on, he collaborated with Lancia in the design of competition cars: Stratos, Beta Montecarlo, LC1, and LC2.

In 1980, he built the first wind tunnel in his company, with which he developed cars that obtained victories in the U.S. and the whole of Europe. From 1988 to 1992, Dallara supplied chassis to the Scuderia Italia in Formula 1. From 1997, he also designed and built chassis for the cars taking part in the American IRL IndyCar Series; from 2005 his company also produced cars for the GP2 and from 2009 cars for the GP3. In the meantime, he was also grappling with decidedly niche road cars. In 2007, he built for KTM the X-Bow, collaborated with Alfa on the design of the 4C in 2013, and in 2017 presented his roadster, the Stradale.

66 • GIAMPAOLO DALLARA, WITH THE BELGIAN DRIVER JACKY ICKX, CAME TO MARANELLO VERY YOUNG, IMMEDIATELY AFTER GRADUATING; BUT AFTER ONLY TWO YEARS WITH FERRARI, HE MOVED TO MASERATI.

67 • AFTER LEAVING MASERATI AND MOVING TO LAMBORGHINI, DALLARA CONTRIBUTED TO DESIGNING HIS V12. IN THE PHOTOGRAPH ABOVE, HE (RIGHT) IS WITH GIOTTO BIZZARRINI AND FERRUCCIO LAMBORGHINI, LEFT AND SECOND FROM LEFT.

MAURO FORGHIERI
(designer)

68 • Mauro Forghieri with the Ferrari 330 P4 designed under him, at the 1967 Brands Hatch 500 Miles, in which his car came second.

In 1959, Mauro Forghieri graduated in Mechanical Engineering from the University of Bologna and, thanks to the good offices of his father, who was one of the most authoritative and respected mechanics of the Ferrari racing department, he too was appointed to the racing department directed by Carlo Chiti, at the same time as Giampaolo Dallara. Forghieri was responsible for engines, Dallara for chassis.

At the end of 1961, Chiti left Ferrari and Dallara moved to Maserati, and thus Enzo Ferrari appointed Forghieri as manager of the technical department for racing cars.

The first victory in Formula 1 for a car developed under his responsibility came at the German GP in 1963.

In 1968, during the Belgian GP, Forghieri introduced the first wings into Formula 1, launching an authentic revolution in the aerodynamics and shape of racing cars.

Then in the 1970s he designed the one-seater in the 312 series (in particular the world champion 312 T, T2, and T4 with cross-mounted gearbox) and at the beginning of the 1980s introduced turbo engines, with which the Scuderia won the constructors' world title in 1982 and 1983.

Under his leadership, Ferrari won 54

GPs, 4 Drivers' Championships, and 7 Constructors' Championships (the last of which was in 1972), while in 1969 the 212 won the European Hill Climb Championship.

He left Ferrari in 1987 to go to Lamborghini Engineering, where he designed a V12 that took part in the 1989 Formula 1 on the Larrousse one-seater. In 1992, he became technical director of the re-formed Bugatti, which he left in 1994 to co-found the Oral Engineering Group, an engineering design company through which he was also responsible for the commission for building the BMW Formula 1 naturally aspirated engine.

69 • FORGHIERI AGAIN AT BRANDS HATCH, THIS TIME IN 1978 WITH THE FORMULA 1 FERRARI 312 T3 DRIVEN BY CARLOS REUTEMANN. THE ARGENTINIAN CAME AN UNSPECTACULAR EIGHTH.

SERGIO PININFARINA
(entrepreneur, designer)

Following in the footsteps of his cousin, the Formula 1 champion Nino Farina, in 1966 Sergio Pininfarina became the executive president of the family car-body business on the death of his father Battista, who had been its founder in 1930. Pinin, the nickname his father was called by, was added to the original surname Farina in 1961, by a decree of President of Italy Giovanni Gronchi.

Sergio graduated in Mechanical Engineering from the Politecnico di Torino in 1950, after which he undertook further studies in the United Kingdom and the United States. Thanks to his mediation, a meeting took place between his padre Battista and the Drake: from this, a collaborative venture was formed which would produce over 100 Ferraris with the Pininfarina name.

Pininfarina would become famous in all the world in the 1950s, thanks to the elegance of its designs and also for avant-garde design; it collaborated with all the most famous world automobile brands.

Sergio Pininfarina was aware of safety problems and also encouraged studies and research in this field: in 1963, he developed the Sigma PF, a car-body study for mid-size cars, and in 1969 the Sigma

Grand Prix, a one-seater concept for Formula 1 with a Ferrari engine featuring original solutions for active and passive safety.

In the 1980s, Pininfarina recognized the importance of aerodynamics and concentrated on improving cars from this point of view.

In 1991 in Detroit, he was awarded the Designer Lifetime Achievement Award as the best automobile designer in the world.

Together with his sporting activity, he went into politics and was elected in the European elections of 1979 as a PLI MEP, but he resigned in 1988 when he became president of Confindustria; he remained in this role until 1992. In 2005, he was appointed Life Senator by the Italian president, Carlo Azeglio Ciampi.

70 • SERGIO PININFARINA (RIGHT) DISCUSSING A POINT WITH HIS BROTHER-IN-LAW RENZO CARLI, THE DIRECTOR-GENERAL AND CEO OF THE FAMILY COMPANY.

71 • BATTISTA FARINA, KNOWN AS "PININ," WITH HIS SON SERGIO. THE FOUNDER OF THE DYNASTY DESERVES CREDIT FOR BEGINNING THE COLLABORATION WITH FERRARI, WHICH STILL CONTINUES.

LEONARDO FIORAVANTI
(designer, entrepreneur)

Leonardo Fioravanti studied Mechanical Engineering at the Politecnico di Milano, specializing in aerodynamics. In 1964 he was hired at Pininfarina, and in the next 24 years he designed, on behalf of this company, some of the most beautiful and sought-after Ferraris of all time. He became one of the historic designers: Dino 206, 365 Daytona, P5, P6, 512 BB, 365 GT4 2+2, 308 GTB, 328, 288 GTO, and 348. He also became chief executive officer at Pininfarina and general manager of the research department.

In 1987, he founded his company—Fioravanti s.r.l.—which was initially an architectural practice that specialized in designing buildings in Japan.

Then in 1988 he moved to the Fiat Group, where he stayed for three years. At the beginning, he was deputy general manager of Ferrari and CEO of Ferrari Engineering, and from 1989 he was director in charge of the style center for Fiat, Alfa Romeo, and Lancia.

In 1991, the company founded by Leonardo Fioravanti began to design road cars, and in 1993 it began to collaborate with the Fiat

Group to create some Alfa Romeo, Fiat, and Lancia prototypes.

Fioravanti continues to create prototypes, and he acts as a consultant in the design sector for various automobile constructors. For example, in 1998 he designed the Ferrari F 100 to celebrate the centenary of the Drake's birth; in 2005 he created the Ferrari Superamerica, a cabriolet transformation of the 575M Maranello; and in 2008 he created the Ferrari SP1, of which there was only one. In fact this became the pioneer of the Special Project, formed by Ferrari itself, for the construction of unique "pieces" designed in collaboration with the most famous names in Italian design and intended for very wealthy private customers.

72 • LEONARDO FIORAVANTI WITH THE FERRARI 512 BB (ORIGINALLY 365 GT/4 BB) IN THE DEFINITIVE VERSION. IN THE BACKGROUND IS THE CAR'S PROTOTYPE, WHICH WAS PRESENTED IN 1971.

73 • FIORAVANTI WORKING ON A SKETCH. HE JOINED PININFARINA IN THE MID-SIXTIES, AND IN THE FOLLOWING YEARS DESIGNED SOME OF THE MOST BEAUTIFUL FERRARIS EVER.

CLAY REGAZZONI
(driver)

Gianclaudio Regazzoni began to race at only twenty-four years old when he took part in several time trials in production cars: he moved to Formula 3 in 1965 and to Formula 2 in 1966.

Right from the beginning, he showed himself to be an instinctive and aggressive driver, but one also with a great ability for car preparation thanks to the knowledge he gained in his family's workshop. He won several victories, and in 1969 he took part in some Formula 2 races, also with the Ferrari Dino 166. The year he definitely arrived was 1970. Enzo Ferrari liked Regazzoni very much, and he brought him to Maranello and moved him to Formula 1, where he had his first win at Monza.

In the next two years, Ferrari had poor results, but with Ferrari Regazzoni won the World Sportscar Championship of 1972, the 1,000 km Monza race, and the Kyalami 9-hour race. In 1973, he moved to BRM to join Niki Lauda, who would take him back to Ferrari in 1974. In that year, Regazzoni won only one GP but garnered many placings; in the end, he was runner-up champion of the world, only four points behind. But that was when the Lauda era began. The Swiss Regazzoni was victorious in only one GP in 1975 and one in 1976.

He could not accept the role of second driver, and also his relationship with the team worsened.

Thus, he moved to the newly founded Ensign in 1977 and then to Shadow in 1978. There were two unsatisfying seasons, but in 1979 he came to Williams, which offered him very different prospects. Indeed, he won at Silverstone, giving the team its first victory in Formula 1. Despite this, Williams let him go, and in 1980 he returned to Ensign, but he had a terrible accident at Long Beach which left his legs paralyzed.

Although he was in a wheelchair for the rest of his life, he did not abandon racing and even took part in the Paris-Dakar rally. He died in 2006 in a road accident in which he lost control of his car.

74 • CLAY REGAZZONI SPENT TWO PERIODS OF HIS CAREER AT FERRARI: FROM 1970 TO 1972, AND THEN FROM 1974, THE YEAR WHEN HE WAS RUNNER-UP IN THE FORMULA 1 CHAMPIONSHIP, TO 1976.

75 • REGAZZONI AT THE 1975 ITALIAN GP, WHICH HE WON IN A FERRARI 312 T3. BUT THE WORLD CHAMPION WAS HIS TEAMMATE NIKI LAUDA, WHO CLAY HIMSELF HAD RECOMMENDED TO ENZO FERRARI.

LUCA CORDERO DI MONTEZEMOLO
(driver, manager)

Luca Cordero di Montezemolo belongs to an old noble Piedmont-ese family that for generations served the royal Savoy family. He graduated in Law in 1971 but had a passion for cars and car racing. He made such a good impression in competitions that he joined the official Lancia rally team.

He met Enzo Ferrari after defending him in a radio program against an attack by a listener who accused him of needlessly incurring costs and running risks to take part in motor races. Thus, in 1973, he joined Maranello as the assistant of the "Grand Old Man" in racing management.

Under his management, after eleven barren years, Ferrari returned to dominating Formula One racing, winning the Constructors' Championship from 1975 to 1977 and the Drivers' Championship with Niki Lauda in 1975 and 1977, while failing to win the 1976 championship by a whisker.

Luca left Ferrari in 1977 for other managerial positions, among them director-general of the organizing committee of the 1990 FIFA World Cup, held in Italy that year.

He returned to Maranello in 1991 as president and CEO and in 2000, after 21 years, the Formula One drivers' title returned to

Ferrari with Michael Schumacher. This success was repeated in the following years, because from 2001 to 2004 Ferrari won both the drivers' and constructors' titles. In his two lives at Ferrari, Montezemolo won a total of 19 world titles, the last in 2007 thanks to Kimi Räikkönen.

He also achieved outstanding successes for Ferrari in the economic field, because under his leadership the road cars improved considerably in performance and quality.

Between 2004 and 2010 he was president of Fiat, and between 1997 and 2005 he was head of Maserati. He continued to lead Ferrari until 2014, when he was replaced by Sergio Marchionne.

76 • Luca Cordero di Montezemolo sitting on the pit wall at Monza in 2013. He began his career as a rally driver, and his passion for racing has never diminished.

77 • Montezemolo with the Spanish driver Fernando Alonso during a press conference. The manager from Bologna led Ferrari until 2014.

NIKI LAUDA

(driver)

Andreas Nikolaus Lauda, who was "Niki" for everyone, was born into a wealthy family of Viennese bankers and became passionately interested in racing at a very early age. But his family got in the way of his passion; and in 1968, after dropping out of university, he obtained a bank loan to buy a car and take part in Formula Vee. He then moved to Formula 3 and, with another loan, to Formula 2. He stood out and, as early as 1971, made his debut in Formula 1 with March; he became their official driver the next year. In 1973 he raced with BRM and was noticed by the Drake, who brought him to Maranello in 1974.

Lauda immediately showed that he was very competitive: he won in Spain and the Netherlands, taking as many as nine pole positions. In 1975, the Lauda/Ferrari combination became unbeatable and the drivers' title was already clinched at the Monza GP, with one more race still to run in the season. In the following year, it seemed that history would repeat itself; but during the German GP at the Nürburgring, Lauda had a terrible accident and was trapped in a burning car. His life was saved, but he was in serious condition and missed several races. Miraculously, he began to race again after only six weeks, but in the end lost the title to James Hunt by a single point. In 1977 he regained the title with several races to go, but his relationship with Enzo Ferrari, which had never been idyllic, deteriorated and in 1978 he moved to Brabham-Alfa Romeo.

The car there, however, was not competitive, and so at the end of the 1979 season he decided to retire to concentrate on his airline, Lauda Air. In 1982 he returned to racing with McLaren and in 1984 he won his third World Championship. The next season was unsatisfying, and so he decided to retire permanently in order to go back to his entrepreneurial activity. In the following years, however, he also worked as a television commentator for Formula 1 GPs and collaborated with the Ferrari, Jaguar, and Mercedes Formula 1 teams.

78 • NIKI LAUDA, SEEN IN 1976, CAME TO MARANELLO IN 1974 AND IMMEDIATELY SHOWED WHAT HE COULD DO. HE ONLY NEEDED A YEAR TO SETTLE IN BEFORE HE BECAME FORMULA 1 WORLD CHAMPION IN 1975.

79 • LAUDA ON THE GRID OF THE 1976 GERMAN GP, IN WHICH HE WAS INVOLVED IN A TERRIBLE LIFE-THREATENING ACCIDENT. BUT AFTER SIX WEEKS, HE WAS BACK IN THE ITALIAN GP.

79

GILLES VILLENEUVE
(driver)

Villeneuve's sporting career began with snowmobile races in his native Quebec, and he became world champion in 1971. Then, at the same time, he began to race in cars. He obtained excellent results in Formula Ford and in 1976 won the Formula Atlantic Championships in both Canada and the U.S. The following year, he made his debut in Formula 1 at the British Grand Prix with McLaren. He was recommended by the reigning Formula 1 champion, James Hunt, after the latter had been beaten by Gilles in a minor race. But Ferrari had already been looking for a replacement for Lauda for the last races of the season: the Drake was impressed by what Villeneuve had shown and signed him for Ferrari.

His style of driving was impulsive and fearless, thus exciting for the spectators. It meant that he was involved in spectacular accidents, and this earned him the nickname of "Aviatore" (Aviator).

He had already won his first GP in 1978 in Canada, and at the end of the 1979 season he was runner-up champion of the world with three wins behind his teammate Jody Scheckter. It was in that year that there was the duel with René Arnoux at the French Grand Prix: today this is still considered one of the most intense

moments in the history of Formula 1. 1980 meant nothing but disappointment, but in 1981 he won spectacular successive victories at Monte Carlo and in Spain. However, during qualification sessions for the Belgian Grand Prix of 1982, due to a misunderstanding, he hit the McLaren of Jochen Mass and his Ferrari was knocked airborne for over 100 meters at a speed of some 120–140 mph, then nosediving and disintegrating, leaving an eternal void in the hearts of Ferrari fans and also the Drake's, who declared "My past is full of pain. . . . Now when I look back I see all those I've loved. And among them there is also this great man, Gilles Villeneuve. I loved him."

Jacques, Gilles's eldest son, followed in his father's footsteps, winning the 500 Miglia in Indianapolis and the Kart Championship in 1995 and the Formula 1 in 1997.

80 • A CONCENTRATED EXPRESSION ON THE FACE OF GILLES VILLENEUVE. THE CANADIAN DRIVER CAME TO FERRARI IN 1977 AND IMMEDIATELY SHOWED HIS DARING.

81 • ABOVE, WE SEE VILLENEUVE IN THE 1980 BELGIAN GP AT ZOLDER. HE WAS KILLED IN AN ACCIDENT WHILE TESTING ON THE SAME CIRCUIT TWO YEARS LATER. ENZO FERRARI MOURNED HIM ALMOST AS A SON.

MICHELE ALBORETO

(driver)

Michele Alboreto made his competitive debut in the Formula Monza of 1976 in a one-seater built by himself, but he quickly moved to Formula 3 in 1978 and in 1980 won that European title. Cesare Fiorio, the sporting director, spotted him and included him in the official team in the World Endurance Championship, where he gained four victories between 1981 and 1982. At the same time, he was also prominent in Formula 2, and this earned him a contract with Tyrrell to race in Formula 1 in 1981. He won his first GP at Las Vegas in 1982 and repeated the victory at Long Beach in the following year. This led in 1984 to his driving for Enzo Ferrari, who finally decided to bring an Italian driver to Maranello.

He gained his first pole position and victory in the 1984 Belgian GP at Zolder; but apart from this, his season was disappointing and in the end he came fourth in the championship.

However, in 1985 he won in Canada and, thanks to good results in the previous races, he was first in the rankings. He repeated his success in Germany; but unfortunately, Ferrari changed turbine suppliers: this created great reliability problems, and he would only be second at the end of the season.

In 1986 he was loyal to Ferrari, despite interest from Williams, but this was one of Ferrari's worst years. In the following two years, things went a little better but there

were no victories; so in 1989 he returned to Tyrrell, and later to Lola, Arrows, and Minardi. But he had no luck, and at the end of 1994 he retired from Formula 1.

At this point, he concentrated on DTM (German Touring Car), Indy Car, and World Sportscar Championships, and here he won the Le Mans 24-Hour Race in 1997 with Porsche and the Sebring 12-Hour Race in 2001 with Audi. But it was with Audi that he lost his life in an accident during a test at the Lausitzring, probably because of a tire explosion.

82–83 • MICHELE ALBORETO CAME TO MARANELLO IN 1984 AFTER PROVING HIMSELF WITH TYRRELL. THIS WAS SENSATIONAL BECAUSE AN ITALIAN HAD NOT DRIVEN A FERRARI IN FORMULA 1 FOR ELEVEN YEARS.

83 • ABOVE, WE SEE ALBORETO IN THE 1985 PORTUGUESE GP, IN WHICH HE FINISHED SECOND BEHIND AYRTON SENNA. IN THAT YEAR, HE SEEMED DESTINED TO WIN THE WORLD CHAMPIONSHIP, BUT THEN FERRARI HAD RELIABILITY PROBLEMS.

ALAIN PROST
(driver, constructor)

Alain Marie Pascal Prost, nicknamed "Il Professore" (The Professor) for his approach to races, began with karts at fourteen and, after Formula Renault and Formula 3, entered Formula 1 in 1980 with McLaren; but Renault signed him for 1981. His first victory came from the French GP, followed by the Dutch and Italian GPs.

In 1982 he won in South Africa and Brazil; and in 1983 he won four races; but Nelson Piquet captured the title in the last race. Prost's relationship with Renault declined, and he signed with McLaren. 1983 began very well, with three victories, but at the end he lost the championship to his teammate Niki Lauda by half a point.

In 1985 he won the title thanks to five victories, but above all due to a decline in Alboreto's Ferrari.

In 1986 he was champion again, owing to three wins and mistaken strategic choices by Williams, which had a better-performing car. In 1987 he managed three wins but was only fourth in the final ranking. The next year, McLaren's superiority was overwhelming, but the Frenchman "only" won seven GPs, and the championship went to his teammate Senna, who won eight.

In 1989 Prost won three races and the title, but he was at loggerheads with Senna, and halfway through the season announced his move to Ferrari, which would involve him in the development of the car. In 1990 he won three GPs and led the championship, but he was caught by Senna's McLaren, which in the last race deliberately forced him off the track and won the title.

1991 was disappointing: he argued with sporting director Cesare Fiorio and was left out before the last GP of the season. He took a year off, and in 1993 he returned to Formula 1 with Williams, winning four races in a row and his fourth title. He retired from driving, but from 1997 to 2001 he took part unsuccessfully as a constructor in Formula 1, with his *scuderia* Prost Grand Prix.

From 2003 on, he tested himself in the Andros Trophy on ice, which he won three times.

84–85 • ALAIN PROST (RIGHT) TALKING TO HIS TEAMMATE NIGEL MANSELL DURING THE TESTS IN PORTUGAL BEFORE THE 1990 CHAMPIONSHIP, IN WHICH HE CAME SECOND TO AYRTON SENNA.

JEAN TODT

(co-driver, manager)

A doctor's son, Jean Todt became fascinated by cars and car racing. He began to race in rallies in his father's car, first as a driver and then as a navigator. It was in this role that he got the best results: he was even second in the 1981 World Championship with a Talbot Lotus, due to his great strategic and organizational ability. He very soon stopped racing to manage the Talbot team, under Peugeot.

In 1981 he became sporting director of Peugeot, which he contributed to restoring to glory after a period of crisis. Between 1985 and 2003, he won, among other things, two World Rally Drivers' and two World Rally Constructors' Championships, two Le Mans 24-Hour races, and four Paris-Dakar rallies.

Thanks to these successes, in 1993 he was appointed, as the first foreigner in the role, manager of the *scuderia* by Luca di Montezemolo. His mission was to achieve the world title, which Ferrari had not won since 1979, and at the end of 1995 he decided to sign Michael Schumacher, who at that time had already won two Formula One world titles. Todt and the German driver formed a strong friendship, and in 1999 the World Constructors' Championship returned to Ferrari, as did the drivers' title in 2000, with close seconds in the three previous years.

In his career at Maranello, Todt won five consecutive Formula One world titles with Schumacher (from 2000 to 2004),

six constructors' titles (from 1999 to 2004), and 106 GPs. Nothing of the kind had previously happened in Formula One.

In 2004 Todt was appointed CEO of Ferrari, and thus his responsibilities went well beyond racing direction.

In 2008 he resigned from the CEO post but remained a director of Ferrari until the following year, when he was elected president of Ferrari until the following year, when he was elected president of the Fédération Internationale de l'Automobile (FIA).

86–87 • THE FRENCHMAN JEAN TODT WAS ONE OF THOSE INSTRUMENTAL IN THE FERRARI SPORTING RENAISSANCE AT THE END OF THE NINETIES. TODAY HE IS PRESIDENT OF THE FÉDÉRATION INTERNATIONALE DE L'AUTOMOBILE.

87 • TODT IS CONGRATULATED BY HIS DRIVERS RUBENS BARRICHELLO AND MICHAEL SCHUMACHER AFTER WINNING THE 2001 HUNGARIAN GP, GAINING FOR FERRARI BOTH THE WORLD TITLES.

MICHAEL SCHUMACHER
(driver)

Michael Schumacher's father had a kart track at Kerpen, and this drew him into the world of car racing. In 1984 he became the German junior kart champion, and two years later he had the opportunity to try out a Formula 3 car: he was very fast. In 1990 he joined the Mercedes team and took part successfully in the World Sportscar Championship. He was noticed by Eddie Jordan, who launched him in Formula 1 in the Belgian Grand Prix of 1991. He made an excellent impression, and Benetton straightaway hired him for the next race at Monza, where he immediately won points, finishing fifth. His next success came again in Belgium in 1992, and his third in 1993 in Portugal. But 1994 was his *annus mirabilis*, with seven victories and the world title. In 1995 it went even better because Schumacher won the drivers' title again with nine wins and also the constructors' title for Benetton (thanks also to two wins by his teammate Johnny Herbert).

However, in 1996 Ferrari "stole" him and his sporting director Ross Brawn from Benetton, with the objective of winning the drivers' title again. Ferrari had not won it since 1979. The Ferrari cars' competitiveness increased dramatically, and in 1997 (five victories) and 1998 (six victories) Schumacher was in contention for the title. 1999 brought

Schumacher only two of Ferrari's six victories, but from 2000 to 2004 he had a victorious cycle, five drivers' titles and five constructors' titles, some of which he won with shocking ease.

In 2005 Schumacher only won one GP. In 2006 he won seven, but he was only runner-up and decided to retire. In the following three years he worked as a consultant and tester for Ferrari, and his return to racing seemed imminent. This actually happened in 2010 with Mercedes. But in three years, he was only once on the podium, with a third place in the Canadian GP of 2012. At the end of that year he left racing forever. On December 29, 2013, he was severely injured in a skiing accident, from which today he still has not recovered.

88 • AN ICONIC IMAGE OF MICHAEL SCHUMACHER KISSING HIS CAR. THE GERMAN LEFT FERRARI AND FORMULA I IN 2006. BUT HE RETURNED WITH MERCEDES IN 2010.

89 • SCHUMACHER MOVED FROM BENETTON TO FERRARI IN 1996, AFTER WINNING THE WORLD TITLE IN THE TWO PREVIOUS YEARS. BUT IT WOULD BE THREE SEASONS BEFORE HE WOULD BEGIN HIS STRING OF VICTORIES.

FLAVIO MANZONI
(designer)

Flavio Manzoni began getting interested in automobile design as an architecture student, and he collaborated with specialist magazines by making sketches of the cars that were about to debut. In 1993, after a degree in Industrial Design, he joined the Lancia style center and in three years became its head regarding interiors. In 1999, he moved to SEAT (Sociedad Española de Automóviles de Turismo) in Barcelona, still as head of interiors, but he also worked on some concepts. He returned to Lancia in 2001 as director of the style center, where he created the splendid Fulvia Coupé Concept (never produced), Ypsilon, and Musa.

In 2004 he also became director of the Fiat style center and worked on the Grande Punto, new 500, Fiorino, and Qubo.

From 2006 to 2010, he worked in the Volkswagen group, where he developed a new style image for various brands but also designed the Scirocco, Golf VI, and Golf Plus.

At the beginning of 2010 he joined Ferrari. He started with the FF, followed by the SA Aperta and the F12 Berlinetta, which was the first product of the Maranello style center in collaboration with Pininfarina.

In 2013, it was the turn of the heir to the Enzo, named LaFerrari, followed by all the cars and concepts produced by Maranello until today. Some stand out among them all: F12tdf, GTC4 Lusso, 488 GTB and Spider, California T, 812 Superfast, Portofino, F8 Tributo, and the very recent SF90 Stradale hybrid sportscar, which introduces a new language of style.

In the context of collaboration between Ferrari and the luxury watchmaker Hublot, in 2019 he designed the Classic Fusion Ferrari GT watch.

In 2011, Flavio Manzoni was inducted into the Hall of Fame of automotive design at the Museo Nazionale dell'Automobile in Turin.

In 2019, the University of Sassari conferred on him a degree *in honoris causa* in Philology, Industrial Culture, and Communication.

90–91 • FLAVIO MANZONI BECAME FERRARI'S HEAD OF DESIGN AT THE BEGINNING OF 2010. LITTLE BY LITTLE, HE MADE SUBSTANTIAL CHANGES TO THE STYLE OF FERRARI ROAD CARS BY MODERNIZING THEM, WHILE RESPECTING TRADITION.

SPORTY, ELEGANT, VERSATILE

NEW V8 TURBO ENGINE
3855 cm³ with fuel direct injection

MAXIMUM POWER
560 Hp @ 7500 rpm

POWER 145 cv/l

CONSUMPTION -15%

TABLE HARD TOP

SERGIO MARCHIONNE

(manager)

Sergio Marchionne was born in Italy, but at the age of fourteen he moved to Canada with his family, where he graduated from several different major Canadian universities in Philosophy, Law, and Economics. He worked in various international companies and then moved to Switzerland, where he met Umberto Agnelli, who appointed him to the Fiat board in 2003. The following year, he became CEO and transformed the company, which went from the verge of bankruptcy to being a competitive multinational. The most important year was 2009, when Fiat took 35% of Chrysler without payment. The merger was completed in 2014, with the foundation of FCA (Fiat Chrysler Automobiles), which became the seventh-leading world car manufacturer, including marques of the caliber of Fiat, Alfa Romeo, Maserati, Jeep, Ram, Dodge, and, of course, Ferrari.

In fourteen years, he eliminated the corporate debt (which was 15 billion euro in 2004) and tripled revenues.

There are those who consider him an enlightened leader and an unrivaled point of reference, and there are those who accuse him of moving the group's industrial center of gravity to the United States, of ignoring the labor unions, and of making himself the interpreter of a globalized capitalism.

In 2014, he also—controversially—became the president of Ferrari after Luca Cordero di Montezemolo, and began the process of its separation from FCA: this was completed at the beginning of 2016 with its quotation on Wall Street. Under his management, Ferrari again became competitive in every field. In Formula One, it won twelve GPs; and from 2015, when Marchionne became the head of the *Scuderia*, it won 60 podium positions. On the financial side, the company was worth over 22 billion euro, with record profits reaching 537 million euro in 2017. Piero Ferrari said of him: "He was a Ferrari man who understood Ferrari's soul."

92–93 • SERGIO MARCHIONNE BECAME PRESIDENT OF FERRARI IN 2014. IN TWO YEARS, HE ACHIEVED ITS QUOTATION ON WALL STREET. HE DIED PREMATURELY IN THE SUMMER OF 2018.

· THE CROWN JEWELS : FROM THE 166 INTER TO THE HYBRID 986 HP

CROWN JEWELS : FROM THE 166 INTER TO THE HYBRID 986 HP SF90

JEWELS : FROM THE 166 INTER TO THE HYBRID 986 HP SF90 · The cro

: FROM THE 166 INTER TO THE HYBRID 986 HP SF90 · The crown jewe

THE 166 INTER TO THE HYBRID 986 HP SF90 · The crown jewels : from t

INTER TO THE HYBRID 986 HP SF90 · The crown jewels : from the 166 Int

The crown jewels:
from the 166 Inter to
the hybrid 986 hp SF90

n the 166 Inter to the h

6 Inter to the hybrid 98

he hybrid 986 hp SF9c

· The crown jewels : from the 166 Inter to the hybrid 986 hp SF90 THE CRO

jewels : from the 166 Inter to the hybrid 986 hp SF90 THE CROWN JEWE

from the 166 Inter to the hybrid 986 hp SF90 THE CROWN JEWELS : FRO

166 Inter to the hybrid 986 hp SF90 THE CROWN JEWELS : FROM THE 16

to the hybrid 986 hp SF90 THE CROWN JEWELS : FROM THE 166 INTER 1

brid 986 hp SF90 THE CROWN JEWELS : FROM THE 166 INTER TO THE H

hp SF90 THE CROWN JEWELS : FROM THE 166 INTER TO THE HYBRID 9

0 · The crown jewels : from the 166 Inter to the hybrid 986 hp SF90 · THE

e crown jewels : from the 166 Inter to the hybrid 986 hp SF90 THE CROWN

ewels : from the 166 Inter to the hybrid 986 hp SF90 THE CROWN JEWELS

om the 166 Inter to the hybrid 986 hp SF90 THE CROWN JEWELS : FROM

66 Inter to the hybrid 986 hp SF90 THE CROWN JEWELS : FROM THE 166

the hybrid 986 hp SF90 THE CROWN JEWELS : FROM THE 166 INTER TO

id 986 hp SF90 THE CROWN JEWELS : FROM THE 166 INTER TO THE HY-

SF90 THE CROWN JEWELS : FROM THE 166 INTER TO THE HYBRID 986

E CROWN JEWELS : FROM THE 166 INTER TO THE HYBRID 986 HP SF90

JEWELS : FROM THE 166 INTER TO THE HYBRID 986 HP SF90 · The crown

FROM THE 166 INTER TO THE HYBRID 986 HP SF90 · The crown jewels :

E 166 INTER TO THE HYBRID 986 HP SF90 · The crown jewels : from the

TER TO THE HYBRID 986 HP SF90 · The crown jewels : from the 166 Inter

HE HYBRID 986 HP SF90 · The crown jewels : from the 166 Inter to the hy-

RID 986 HP SF90 · The crown jewels : from the 166 Inter to the hybrid 986

IP SF90 · The crown jewels : from the 166 Inter to the hybrid 986 hp SF90 ·

Design has a certain purity to it. An ability to capture a moment in time, with perfect clarity. The figurative art best able to create a true representation that transcends time. Capturing the essence of things without making any allowances for the changes and transformations wrought by the passage of time, while colors, shapes, and details inevitably change as the years go by. Photography only provides us with a fleeting glimpse of how things were. The physical form of the masterpieces created at Maranello over ninety years has inevitably been modified, transformed, and damaged, losing that essential purity in the collective imagination in the process.

This book is intended as a tribute to the formal perfection of the Prancing Horse marque. As it was. As it still is. Which is destined to remain in the hearts of auto lovers—and not only theirs.

Computer rendering is used to develop the designs of the new millennium. Rendering, the art dear to stylists, designers, and developers, which can provide three-dimensional representations of any object, including cars. It is a tool that goes beyond the limitations of the traditional figurative arts. A car design can now be handled as if it were a precious gem, rotating it this way and that way; observing the changes in its many facets as the light glides over its lines; emphasizing its most hidden beauty; bringing it to life.

Each Ferrari that comes to life in this book by means of this technique is a fragment of the larger mosaic of Prancing Horse history.

Forty-three models are the protagonists of this new edition. Forty-three precious gems, the jewels in the Ferrari crown. From early times up to the present day, first passing through the crucial, epoch-making moments of Enzo Ferrari's life and arriving at Maranello's modern production facility. Milestones in the evolution of technology and design, unique events in the history of the motor car managed by men who have made the Prancing Horse a world brand, making it the strongest brand in the world in rankings of image power, profitability, and company prospect. Ferrari is also synonymous with design, and no book would be complete without special attention being paid to the art of Pininfarina, the principal inspiration for Ferrari style and design since the nineteen-fifties. Series production models, and one-off examples, too. One-off designs where the designer was given a free hand, liberated from production and commercial constraints and governed by artistic imperatives alone. Or sometimes recovering fundamental stylistic elements from the Maranello tradition and transporting them to the present to establish a timeless link between the masterpieces of the past and those of the present. Hallowed series production cars included the 250 California LWB of 1957, one of the most captivating spiders from Maranello; and, of course, the 250 Testa Rossa roadster of the same year. In 1984, the two words of the name became one: Testarossa. The berlinetta that broke all the design rules of the time.

The nineteen-eighties witnessed the arrival of such epoch-making vehicles as the 288 GTO, one of the most stunning Ferraris ever produced. This car pioneered the use of twin turbochargers and is considered to be the spiritual forerunner of the mighty F40, a supercar with a raw, mean look and an awe-inspiring power output to match. The line of extreme performance supercars from Maranello continued with the F50, the Ferrari road car that came the closest to being a Formula One racer. Next up was the Enzo, with a distinctive front end and a monocoque body derived directly from single-seater race cars. Today there are the breathtaking LaFerrari, a hybrid boasting a massive 949 hp (963 cv), and the very recent SF90 Stradale, whose name celebrates the anniversary of the Ferrari brand, while it achieves state-of-the-art technology in combining the traditional engine and the electric engine to touch the monumental limit of 986 hp (1,000 cv).

We will also be looking at some of the cars behind the commercial success of the Prancing Horse marque and feature the "family-size" grand touring 330 GT 2+2 of 1964 and the 308 GTB/GTS, a best seller from 1975. Also featured are the ground-breaking F355 Berlinetta (1994) and its successor, the 360 Modena (1999), and then the 430 (2007), the 458 Italia (2009), and the 488 GTB (2015), radically departing from the technical and stylistic standards of the time.

We have already mentioned the one-off creations tailored to their owner's individual specifications and the limited-edition commemorative models. Here we can name a few. The SP12 EC commissioned by the famous guitarist Eric Clapton. The P540 SuperFast Aperta derived from the 599 GTB Fiorano. The commemorative 550 Barchetta Pininfarina, a design exercise recalling the roadsters of the nineteen-seventies. The pinnacle of creative freedom was reached in 1967 with the striking Modulo, a concept car which deliberately challenged the styling canons of the sixties. Its fundamental, ground-breaking features still influence futuristic concept cars today. Reading this book is a wonderful, evocative journey—through the history, technology, and design of the Maranello marque. But it is also a journey through a culture that goes beyond cars and sport, because for ninety years Ferrari has also had a special place in the hearts of those outside the world of cars and sport. The history of the classic Ferrari red cars. Are you ready to start? Follow us, and you won't be sorry.

FERRARI 166 INTER

1948

Enzo Ferrari took a great liking to the coachbuilder Bodywork Touring. In 1940, he entrusted the building of the Auto Avio Costruzioni 815, his first creation after leaving Alfa Romeo, to this Milan coachbuilder. No surprise, then, that in 1948, when Ferrari decided to build a competition car for the Sport category, he called on Touring once again. Touring had in the meantime become renowned for its super-leggera (super-lightweight) bodywork which combined great structural stiffness with greatly reduced weight.

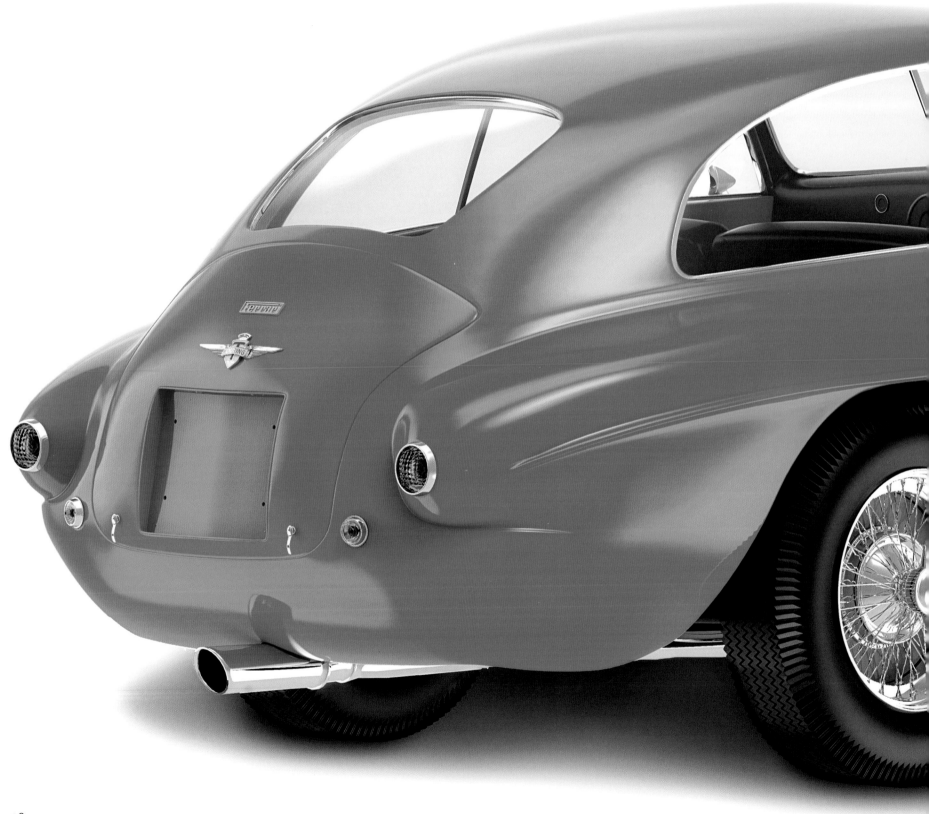

The result was the 166 MM Touring, where the initials MM stand for Mille Miglia, the celebrated road race which in the years to come was to see a string of victories by cars from Maranello. The 166 MM Touring had barchetta bodywork and was powered by a front-mounted 60° V12 with a displacement of 122 cu in (1,995 cc). The 166 Inter was the road-going, grand-touring version. The buzz created by Ferrari's successes in competition quickly attracted the interest of leading coachbuilders, including Ghia, Vignale, and Stabilimenti Farina.

Farina and Bertone both offered a cabriolet version with a fabric soft top. The vehicles of the Inter series were originally designed as road cars, but numerous owners used them with some success in competition events: this despite the fact that the bodywork was heavier than that of race cars. The 166 MM Barchetta racer, for example, weighed 1,433 lb (650 kg), while its roadgoing cousin, the 166 Inter Berlinetta, tipped the scales at 1,984 lb (900 kg). A total of 37 Inters were built between 1948 and 1950.

TECHNICAL DATA

ENGINE

Type:	Front, longitudinal
Cylinders:	V12 (60°)
Bore x stroke:	2.36 x 2.31 in (60.0 x 58.8 mm)
Displacement:	122 cu in (1,995 cc)
Maximum power:	90 HP at 5,600 rpm
Maximum torque:	---
Valve actuation:	Single overhead camshaft per cylinder bank
Valves:	Two per cylinder
Fuel feed:	Single Weber 32 DCF carburetor
Ignition:	One spark plug per cylinder, twin coils
Cooling:	Water-cooled
Lubrication:	Wet sump

TRANSMISSION

Drive:	Rear-wheel drive
Clutch:	Dry single-plate
Gearbox:	Manual, 5-speed + reverse

CHASSIS

Bodywork:	Two-seater berlinetta and barchetta – 2+2 coupé
Frame:	Tubular steel, ladder type
Front suspension:	Independent, unequal-length wishbones with transverse leaf spring and hydraulic shock absorbers
Rear suspension:	Live axle, semi-elliptic longitudinal leaf springs, hydraulic shock absorbers and anti-roll bar
Steering:	Worm and sector

Front/rear brakes:	Drums		Height:	—
Wheels:	15-in wire wheels with 5.50 x 15 tires front and rear		Weight:	1984 lb (900 kg) (berlinetta)
			Fuel tank capacity:	19 gal (72 liters)

DIMENSIONS AND WEIGHT

Wheelbase:	103.1 in (2,620 mm)
Front/rear track:	49.2/47.2 in (1,250/1,200 mm)
Length:	—
Width:	—

PERFORMANCE

Top speed:	93 mph (150 km/h)
Acceleration 0 to 60 mph (0 to 100 km/h):	—
Weight/power ratio:	22 lb/hp (10.0 kg/hp)

This car was designed for sunny California, and it was Luigi Chinetti, U.S. importer of Maranello cars, who convinced Enzo Ferrari that the idea was a good one. Scaglietti Bodyworks produced one of the most attractive spiders in the history of the Prancing Horse marque. The body was mainly steel with aluminum opening panels (doors, hood, and trunk). Some versions, designed for competition, were made entirely of aluminum. The car was derived from the 250 GT Berlinetta and shared the same Tour de France version of the 183 cu in (3-liter) V12 engine. The first models featured plexiglass fairings on the headlight units.

In 1958, the second version had open units and more pronounced wheel arches. Another restyling in 1959 introduced engine-bay exhaust vents with three vertical strips on the front fenders, chromed headlight rings, and a raised air intake in the center of the hood. The re-styled cars had disc brakes in place of the drum-brake setup of earlier versions. The long-wheelbase (102 in/2,600 mm) version was produced until 1960, when it was replaced by the short-wheelbase (94 in/2,400 mm) spider, based on the SWB berlinetta, which continued to be produced until 1962. Power of the V12 was stepped up to 280 hp. A removable hard top was available for both models.

FERRARI 250 CALIFORNIA LWB

1957

TECHNICAL DATA

ENGINE

Type:	Front, longitudinal
Cylinders:	V12 (60°)
Bore x stroke:	2.87 x 2.31 in (73.0 x 58.8 mm)
Displacement:	180 cu in (2,953 cc)
Maximum power:	240 hp (260 hp from 1958) at 7,000 rpm
Maximum torque:	182 lb-ft (25.2 kgm) at 5,500 rpm
Valve actuation:	Single overhead camshaft per cylinder bank
Valves:	Two per cylinder
Fuel feed:	Three Weber 36 DCL3 carburetors
Ignition:	One spark plug per cylinder, twin coils
Cooling:	Water-cooled
Lubrication:	Wet sump

TRANSMISSION

Drive:	Rear-wheel drive
Clutch:	Twin-plate
Gearbox:	Manual, 4-speed + reverse

CHASSIS

Bodywork:	Two-seater spider
Frame:	Tubular steel, ladder type
Front suspension:	Independent, unequal-length wishbones, coil springs with Houdaille hydraulic shock absorbers
Rear suspension:	Live axle, semi-elliptic longitudinal leaf springs, Houdaille hydraulic shock absorbers
Steering:	Worm and sector
Front/rear brakes:	Drums, discs from 1959
Wheels:	16-in wire wheels with 6.00 x 16 tires

DIMENSIONS AND WEIGHT

Wheelbase:	102.4 in (2,600 mm)
Front/rear track:	53.3/53.1 in (1,354/1,349 mm)
Length:	173.2 in (4,400 mm)
Width:	65.0 in (1,650 mm)
Height:	55.1 in (1,400 mm)
Weight:	2,204 lb (1,000 kg) (2,370 lb/1,075 kg from 1959)
Fuel tank capacity:	26 gal (100 liters) (36 gal/136 liters from 1959)

PERFORMANCE

Top speed:	157–167 mph (252–268 km/h)
Acceleration 0 to 60 mph (0 to 100 km/h):	8.7 seconds
Weight/power ratio:	9.19–9.91 lb/hp (4.17–4.13 kg/hp)

FERRARI 250
TESTA ROSSA

1957

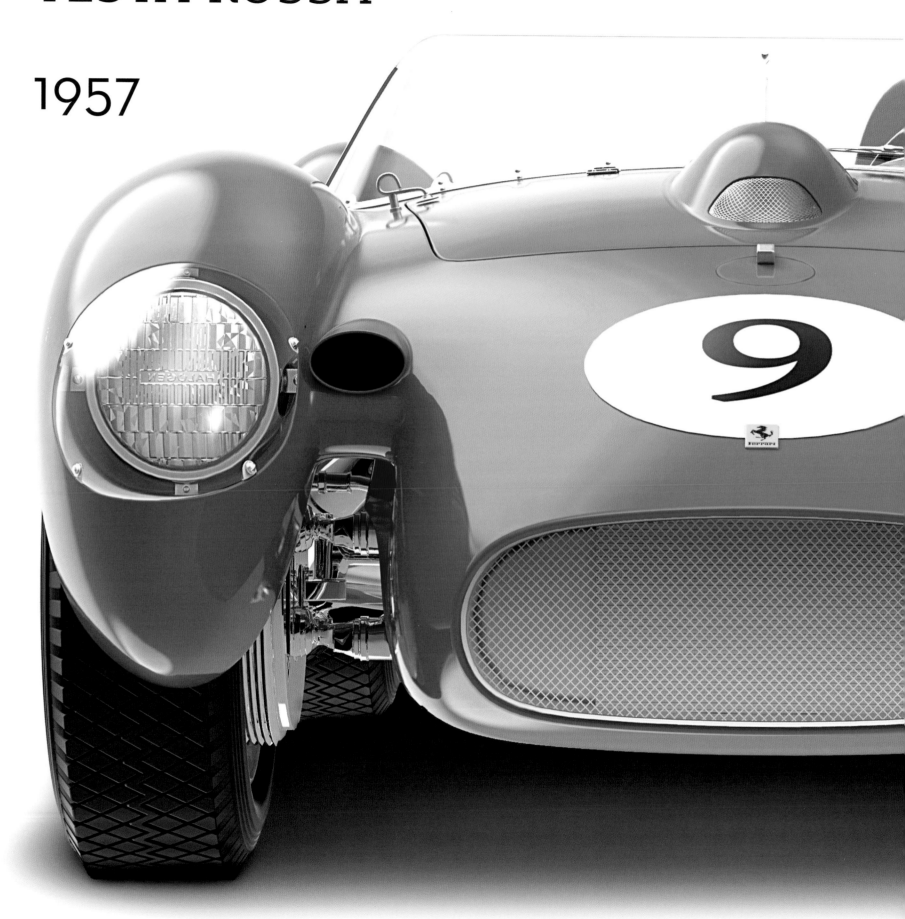

In disguise. This is how one of the most illustrious Ferraris of all time appeared at its debut. The 250 Testa Rossa made its debut at the 1000-kilometer race at the Nürburgring circuit in Germany, masquerading in the colors of a private American team while awaiting delivery to racing customers. Teams were already racing the 500 TRC but were looking for a car with a more powerful engine that retained the great handling of the 4-cylinder 500 TRC barchetta. The new car was the result of changes to FIA regulations in 1958 which introduced a 183 cu in (3-liter) limit for prototypes. The 250 TR had the same 183 cu in (3-liter) V12 as the 250 GT Competizione berlinetta, increased from 260 to 300 hp.

This power upgrade was made possible by increasing the compression ratio from 8.5:1 to 9.8:1 and by fitting six Weber carburetors in place of the three original units. The bodywork by Scaglietti was similar in appearance to the 500 TR. Both cars share the same TR suffix where TR stands for Testa Rossa or "red head," a reference to the fact that the valve covers were painted red. The 250 TR was 4 in (100 mm) longer than the 500 TR and had a characteristic protruding hood shaped to house the intake trumpets of the Weber twin-choke carburetors. The car won the Manufacturers' World Championship in 1958 and had a long and extraordinary racing career which only came to an end in 1962.

TECHNICAL DATA

ENGINE

Type:	Front, longitudinal
Cylinders:	V12 (60°)
Bore x stroke:	2.87 x 2.31 in (73.0 x 58.8 mm)
Displacement:	180 cu in (2,953 cc)
Maximum power:	300 hp at 7,000 rpm
Maximum torque:	221 lb-ft (30.6 kgm) at 5,500 rpm
Valve actuation:	Single overhead camshaft per cylinder bank
Valves:	Two per cylinder
Fuel feed:	Six Weber 38 DCN carburetors

Ignition:	One spark plug per cylinder, twin coils
Cooling:	Water-cooled
Lubrication:	Wet sump

TRANSMISSION

Drive:	Rear-wheel drive
Clutch:	Twin-plate
Gearbox:	Manual, 4-speed + reverse

CHASSIS

Bodywork:	Two-seater spider
Frame:	Tubular steel trellis

Front suspension:	Independent, unequal-length wishbones, coil springs with Houdaille hydraulic shock absorbers
Rear suspension:	Live axle, coil springs, Houdaille hydraulic shock absorbers
Steering:	Worm and sector
Front/rear brakes:	Drums, discs from 1959
Wheels:	Front: 15-in wire wheels with 5.50 x 15 tires. Rear: 16-in wire wheels with 6.00 x 16 tires

DIMENSIONS AND WEIGHT

Wheelbase:	92.5 in (2,350 mm)

Front/rear track:	51.5/51.2 in (1,308/1,300 mm)
Length:	164.5 in (4,178 mm)
Width:	61.0 in (1,549 mm)
Height:	39.9 in (1,013 mm)
Weight:	1,764 lb (800 kg)
Fuel tank capacity:	37 gal (140 liters)

PERFORMANCE

Top speed:	168 mph (270 km/h)
Acceleration 0 to 60 mph (0 to 100 km/h):	—
Weight/power ratio:	5.89 lb/hp (2.67 kg/hp)

FERRARI 250 GTO

1962

One of the most victorious and attractive Ferraris ever built. The 250 GTO (Gran Turismo Omologato) was designed by Ferrari to combat (successfully, as it turned out) the emerging foreign competition for the Manufacturers' World Championship title in the nineteen-sixties. Developed by Giotto Bizzarrini and his design team, the car was nicknamed "the duck" because of its low, sinuous body line with a cut-off tail topped by a small spoiler. The car combined the charisma of a grand tourer with the performance of a thoroughbred sportscar. However, under the hood things were anything but revolutionary. The engine was the well-known 183 cu in (3-liter) V12 of the 250 Testa Rossa, with the only difference being the dry-sump lubrication used in place of the original wet-sump type. The tubular steel chassis with longitudinal members and crossbraces was derived from the 250 GT SWB, slightly stiffened but with the same 94.5 in (2,400 mm) wheelbase. Built by Scaglietti with aluminum bodywork, it featured four disc brakes and, most notably, a new manual 5-speed gearbox. In 1962, the transfer of the manufacturers' championship to the GT category gave Ferrari a hat trick of victories. Competition success continued more or less unabated until 1964, the last year of the car's competition career, when the 250 GTO began to suffer from the competition of the AC Cobra powered by a hefty 427 cu in (7-liter) Ford V8. This was one of the few cars from a small production run which was equally at home on the road and on the race track. Thirty-six were built, and the car now has a cult following among collectors.

TECHNICAL DATA

ENGINE

Type:	Front, longitudinal
Cylinders:	V12 (60°)
Bore x stroke:	2.87 x 2.31 in (73.0 x 58.8 mm)
Displacement:	180 cu in (2,953 cc)
Maximum power:	300 hp at 7,400 rpm
Maximum torque:	221 lb-ft (30.6 kgm) at 5,500 rpm
Valve actuation:	Single overhead camshaft per cylinder bank
Valves:	Two per cylinder
Fuel feed:	Six Weber 38 DCN carburetors
Ignition:	One spark plug per cylinder, single coil
Cooling:	Water-cooled
Lubrication:	Dry sump

TRANSMISSION

Drive:	Rear-wheel drive
Clutch:	Dry single-plate
Gearbox:	Manual, 5-speed + reverse

CHASSIS

Bodywork:	Two-seater berlinetta
Frame:	Tubular steel, ladder type
Front suspension:	Independent, unequal-length wishbones, coil springs, telescopic shock absorbers, anti-roll bar
Rear suspension:	Live axle, longitudinal leaf springs, coil springs, and telescopic shock absorbers
Steering:	Worm and sector
Front/rear brakes:	Disc
Wheels:	15-in wire wheels with 6.00 x 15 (front) and 7.00 x 15 (rear) tires

DIMENSIONS AND WEIGHT

Wheelbase:	94.5 in (2,400 mm)
Front/rear track:	53.3/53.1 in (1,354/1,350 mm)
Length:	170.3 in (4,325 mm)
Width:	63.0 in (1,600 mm)
Height:	47.6 in (1,210 mm)
Weight:	1,940 lb (880 kg)
Fuel tank capacity:	34 gal (130 liters)

PERFORMANCE

Top speed:	174 mph (280 km/h)
Acceleration 0 to 60 mph (0 to 100 km/h):	5.6 seconds
Weight/power ratio:	6.43 lb/hp (2.93 kg/hp)

FERRARI 250 GTL

1962

Body styled by Pininfarina and built by Scaglietti. This was a luxury berlinetta with a decidedly sporting character. GTL stands for Gran Turismo Lusso (Grand Touring Luxury), while 250 indicates the cubic capacity of each of the 12 cylinders. The interior was luxurious and designed with some attention. Mechanically, the car was state-of-the-art and undoubtedly Ferrari's best front-engine GT of the period.

The car had the same 183 cu in (3-liter) V12 engine as the 250 GT Competizione berlinetta, delivering 240 hp and fed by three Weber carburetors. The tubular steel chassis with longitudinal members and crossbraces was derived from the 250 GT SWB with a 94.5 in (2,400 mm) wheelbase and was the same frame as the stiffened version on the 250 GTO. The car's appearance was striking, with a distinctive shark's-mouth front end, chromed air intake in the center of the hood, very slim door pillars, and a cut-off recessed tail panel. The independent front suspension featured a robust wishbone and pushrod system, while the live-axle rear suspension had longitudinal leaf springs. The four disc brakes testify to the car's sporting origins. Approximately 350 cars of this model were built, and they are often described as the swan song for Maranello's 183 cu in (3-liter) V12. Although the 250 GT Lusso was designed and built as a road car, some private owners took them into competition. One finished thirteenth in the Targa Florio in 1964.

TECHNICAL DATA

ENGINE

Type:	Front, longitudinal
Cylinders:	V12 (60°)
Bore x stroke:	2.87 x 2.31 in (73.0 x 58.8 mm)
Displacement:	180 cu in (2,953 cc)
Maximum power:	240 hp at 7,500 rpm
Maximum torque:	–
Valve actuation:	Single overhead camshaft per cylinder bank
Valves:	Two per cylinder

Fuel feed:	Three Weber 36 DCS carburetors
Ignition:	One spark plug per cylinder, twin coils
Cooling:	Water-cooled
Lubrication:	Wet sump

TRANSMISSION

Drive:	Rear-wheel drive
Clutch:	Dry single-plate
Gearbox:	Manual, 4-speed + reverse

CHASSIS

Bodywork:	Two-seater berlinetta

Frame:	Tubular steel, ladder type
Front suspension:	Independent, unequal-length wishbones, coil springs, telescopic shock absorbers, anti-roll bar
Rear suspension:	Live axle, longitudinal leaf springs, coil springs and telescopic shock absorbers
Steering:	Worm and sector
Front/rear brakes:	Disc
Wheels:	15-in wire wheels with 6.50 x 15 tires front and rear

DIMENSIONS AND WEIGHT

Wheelbase:	94.5 in (2,400 mm)
Front/rear track:	54.9/54.6 in (1,395/1,387 mm)
Length:	173.6 in (4,410 mm)
Width:	68.9 in (1,750 mm)
Height:	50.8 in (1,290 mm)
Weight:	2,249 lb (1,020 kg)
Fuel tank capacity:	30 gal (114 liters)

PERFORMANCE

Top speed:	149 mph (240 km/h)
Acceleration 0 to 60 mph (0 to 100 km/h):	—
Weight/power ratio:	9.37 lb/hp (4.25 kg/hp)

Constructed by the Scaglietti bodyworks and styled by Pininfarina, this was the last Ferrari berlinetta to be equipped with a single overhead camshaft per cylinder bank.

The car continued the Ferrari tradition of a front-mounted V12 engine, a traditional approach in a period when other European manufacturers had for some time been considering mid-engine and rear-engine configurations. The only modern concessions were the incorporation of technical spinoffs from the race track. The gearbox and differential were combined and moved to the rear in a transaxle assembly. This was also the first production Ferrari to boast independent suspension on both axles.

The very responsive handling of the vehicle can be attributed not only to the transaxle solution, which enabled a balanced distribution of the weight between the front and rear axles, but also to the lowering of the center of gravity enabled by the use of dry-sump lubrication. The styling of the 275 GTB was also quite distinctive: it had a very long nose, faired headlights, and a truncated tail topped by a kind of spoiler. In 1966, a version was developed with a 4-camshaft engine delivering 300 hp.

This version, known as the GTB/4, can be identified by the raised section along the hood. There was also a spider version, the 275 GTS, and a competition model, the 275 GTB/C.

FERRARI 275 GTB

1964

TECHNICAL DATA

ENGINE

Type:	Front, longitudinal
Cylinders:	V12 (60°)
Bore x stroke:	3.03 x 2.31 in (77.0 x 58.8 mm)
Displacement:	201 cu in (3,286 cc)
Maximum power:	280 hp at 7,600 rpm
Maximum torque:	217 lb-ft (30.0 kgm) at 5,000 rpm
Valve actuation:	Single overhead camshaft per cylinder bank
Valves:	Two per cylinder
Fuel feed:	Three Weber 40 DCN/3 carburetors
Ignition:	One spark plug per cylinder, twin coils
Cooling:	Water-cooled
Lubrication:	Dry sump

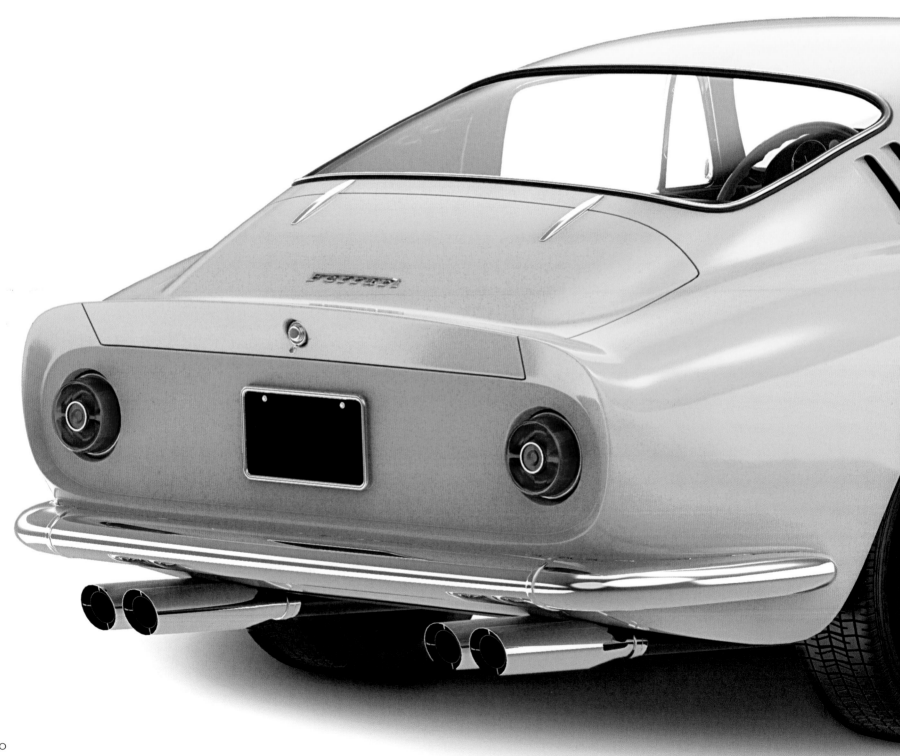

TRANSMISSION

Drive:	Rear-wheel drive
Clutch:	Dry single-plate
Gearbox:	Manual, 5-speed + reverse

CHASSIS

Bodywork:	Two-seater berlinetta
Frame:	Tubular steel
Front suspension:	Independent, unequal-length wishbones, coil springs, telescopic shock absorbers, anti-roll bar
Rear suspension:	Independent, unequal-length wishbones, coil springs, telescopic shock absorbers, anti-roll bar
Steering:	Worm and roller

Front/rear brakes:	Disc
Wheels:	14-in light alloy rims with 205/70 tires front and rear

DIMENSIONS AND WEIGHT

Wheelbase:	94.5 in (2,400 mm)
Front/rear track:	54.2/54.8 in (1,377/1,393 mm)
Length:	170.3 in (4,325 mm)
Width:	67.9 in (1,725 mm)
Height:	49.0 in (1,245 mm)
Weight:	2,425 lb (1,100 kg)
Fuel tank capacity:	25 gal (94 liters)

PERFORMANCE

Top speed:	155 mph (250 km/h)
Acceleration 0 to 60 mph (0 to 100 km/h):	—
Weight/power ratio:	8.66 lb/hp (3.93 kg/hp)

FERRARI 330 GT 2+2

1964

In 1960, the Ferrari 250 GT 2+2 introduced the idea of the family-size grand tourer, a sports car that could seat four people. This successful coupé was followed by the 330 GT 2+2. Designed by Pininfarina, the 330 GT 2+2 originally had a dual-headlight arrangement, a feature particularly popular on the U.S. market at the time. A re-styling in 1965 saw the dual headlights replaced by a more conventional sports configuration with single headlights. The re-styling also saw the introduction of other changes: The manual 4-speed gearbox with overdrive was replaced with a 5-speed gearbox. Both units were mechanical, of course. The traditional Borrani wire wheels gave way to alloy rims with a more modern design. The 330 GT 2+2 was longer and heavier than the 250 GT 2+2. It was 191 in or 4,840 mm long (185 in/4,700 mm), had a wheelbase of 104 in or 2,650 mm (102 in/2,600 mm) and weighed in at 3,042 lb/1,380 kg (2,821 lb/1,280 kg); the figures in parentheses are for the 250 GT 2+2. The major difference was the increase in displacement of the front-mounted, 24-valve V12, which grew from 180 to 242 cu in (2,953 cc to 3,967 cc). This engine was derived from the 400 Superamerica unit and delivered 300 hp. Independent front-wheel suspension contrasted with the more traditional live-axle suspension arrangement on the rear. Like other luxury coupés of the time, this car was available with air conditioning, power steering, and electric window winders as optionals. Enzo Ferrari himself used the car for a long time, contributing to its development. It was "retired" in 1967 to make way for the 365 GT 2+2.

TECHNICAL DATA

ENGINE

Type:	Front, longitudinal
Cylinders:	V12 (60°)
Bore x stroke:	3.03 x 2.80 in (77.0 x 71.0 mm)
Displacement:	242 cu in (3,967 cc)
Maximum power:	300 hp at 6,600 rpm
Maximum torque:	288 lb-ft (39.8 kgm) at 5,000 rpm
Valve actuation:	Single overhead camshaft per cylinder bank
Valves:	Two per cylinder
Fuel feed:	Three Weber 40 DCZ/6 carburetors
Ignition:	One spark plug per cylinder, twin coils
Cooling:	Water-cooled
Lubrication:	Wet sump

TRANSMISSION

Drive:	Rear-wheel drive
Clutch:	Dry single-plate
Gearbox:	Manual, 4-speed + overdrive + reverse (5-speed + reverse from 1965)

CHASSIS

Bodywork:	2+2 coupé
Frame:	Tubular steel
Front suspension:	Independent, unequal-length wishbones, coil springs, telescopic shock absorbers, anti-roll bar
Rear suspension:	Live axle, longitudinal push rod and leaf springs, coil springs and telescopic shock absorbers
Steering:	Worm and roller
Front/rear brakes:	Disc
Wheels:	15-in wire wheels (light alloy rims from 1966) with 205/70 tires front and rear

DIMENSIONS AND WEIGHT

Wheelbase:	104.3 in (2,650 mm)
Front/rear track:	55.0/54.7 in (1,397/1,389 mm)
Length:	190.5 in (4,840 mm)
Width:	67.5 in (1,715 mm)
Height:	53.5 in (1,360 mm)
Weight:	3,042 lb (1,380 kg)
Fuel tank capacity:	24 gal (90 liters)

PERFORMANCE

Top speed:	152 mph (245 km/h)
Acceleration 0 to 60 mph (0 to 100 km/h):	—
Weight/power ratio:	10.14 lb/hp (4.60 kg/hp)

FERRARI
330 P3

1966

This car seemed to have everything it takes to be a winner. But it didn't win. The World Sports Prototype Championship in 1966 was dominated by the Ford GT40. Ferrari was beaten at the Le Mans 24 Hours. This was a series of unhappy events that Ferrari had not experienced since 1959. Not at all pleased with the defeat, Enzo Ferrari ordered a radical redesign of the 330 P3, even though the car was anything but obsolete. The result was the 330 P4, introduced in 1967. But first let's take a step back in time. The 330 P3, an evolution of the

330 P2, featured Drogo bodywork and had a new tubular chassis-frame with aluminum plate reinforcement and a fiberglass underbody. The unequal-length wishbone suspension at the front and the rear was the same as before.

The mid-mounted 242 cu in (3,967 cc) V12 was redesigned and considerably lightened, weighing in at 66 lb (30 kg) less than the V12 of the previous generation. The fuel-feed system underwent a major change, as Lucas indirect fuel injection took the place of the tradi-tional battery of six Weber carburetors. The upgrade boosted the power from 410 hp on the P2 to 420 hp. The manual 5-speed gearbox was a German ZF unit. This was later to be replaced on the 330 P4 by a gearbox made in-house at Maranello. The P4 was also to benefit from another innovation: 3 valves per cylinder, two for the intake and one for the exhaust. Only three examples of the P3 were built. These were rebodied by Drogo in P4 style to become the 412 P and were then supplied to private teams.

TECHNICAL DATA

ENGINE

Type:	Central, longitudinal
Cylinders:	V12 (60°)
Bore x stroke:	3.03 x 2.80 in (77.0 x 71.0 mm)
Displacement:	242 cu in (3,967 cc)
Maximum power:	420 hp at 8,000 rpm
Maximum torque:	–
Valve actuation:	Twin overhead camshafts per bank
Valves:	Two per cylinder
Fuel feed:	Lucas indirect injection
Ignition:	Twin spark plugs per cylinder, twin coils

Cooling:	Water-cooled
Lubrication:	Dry sump

TRANSMISSION

Drive:	Rear-wheel drive
Clutch:	Multi-plate
Gearbox:	Manual, 5-speed + reverse

CHASSIS

Bodywork:	Two-seater berlinetta/spider
Frame:	Tubular steel with aluminum plate reinforcement
Front suspension:	Independent, unequal-length wishbones, coil springs, telescopic shock absorbers, anti-roll bar

Rear suspension:	Independent, unequal-length wishbones, coil springs, telescopic shock absorbers, anti-roll bar
Steering:	Rack and pinion
Front/rear brakes:	Disc
Wheels:	15-in magnesium alloy rims with 5.50 x 15 (front) and 7.00 x 15 (rear) tires

DIMENSIONS AND WEIGHT

Wheelbase:	94.5 in (2,400 mm)
Front/rear track:	57.6/56.3 in (1,462/1,431 mm)
Length:	164.2 in (4,170 mm)
Width:	70.1 in (1,780 mm)
Height:	37.4 in (950 mm)
Weight:	1,876 lb (851 kg)

Fuel tank capacity:	30 gal (114 liters)

PERFORMANCE

Top speed:	193 mph (310 km/h)
Acceleration 0 to 60 mph (0 to 100 km/h):	—
Weight/power ratio:	4.48 lb/hp (2.03 kg/hp)

FERRARI MODULO

1967

A breathtaking dream car. Too much of a dream to ever enter production. Developed on the basis of a 512 S competition prototype, this concept car was designed by Pininfarina with the deliberate aim of challenging the styling canons of the sixties. It certainly achieved this with a one-box design where the bodywork consisted of two shells, one on top of the other, separated by a straight groove along the waistline. The front end, roof, and rear engine

cover form a single arching curve. The rear wheels are faired into the bodywork with the fairing partly open to reveal the wheel, thereby creating a cylindrical motif. Access to the passenger compartment was by sliding the entire canopy, including the windshield, forward along special guides. Unveiled at the Geneva Motor Show in 1970, only one model was ever built. It won 22 international design awards, was selected to represent the best of Italian coach-

building at the 1970 Osaka Expo, and was displayed as an ambassador for Italian design in Mexico City in 1971. This was a working car powered by a mid-engine—a 48-valve, 305 cu in (5-liter) V12 developing 550 hp fitted with a manual 5-speed gearbox. The chassis frame was tubular steel as per the current practice of the time. It had a pushrod wishbone-type suspension. Performance figures were never published.

TECHNICAL DATA

ENGINE

Type:	Central, longitudinal
Cylinders:	V12 (60°)
Bore x stroke:	3.43 x 2.76 in (87.0 x 70.0 mm)
Displacement:	305 cu in (4,994 cc)
Maximum power:	550 hp at 8,500 rpm
Maximum torque:	—
Valve actuation:	Twin overhead camshafts per bank
Valves:	Four per cylinder
Fuel feed:	Lucas indirect injection
Ignition:	One spark plug per cylinder, electronic
Cooling:	Water-cooled
Lubrication:	Dry sump

TRANSMISSION

Drive:	Rear-wheel drive

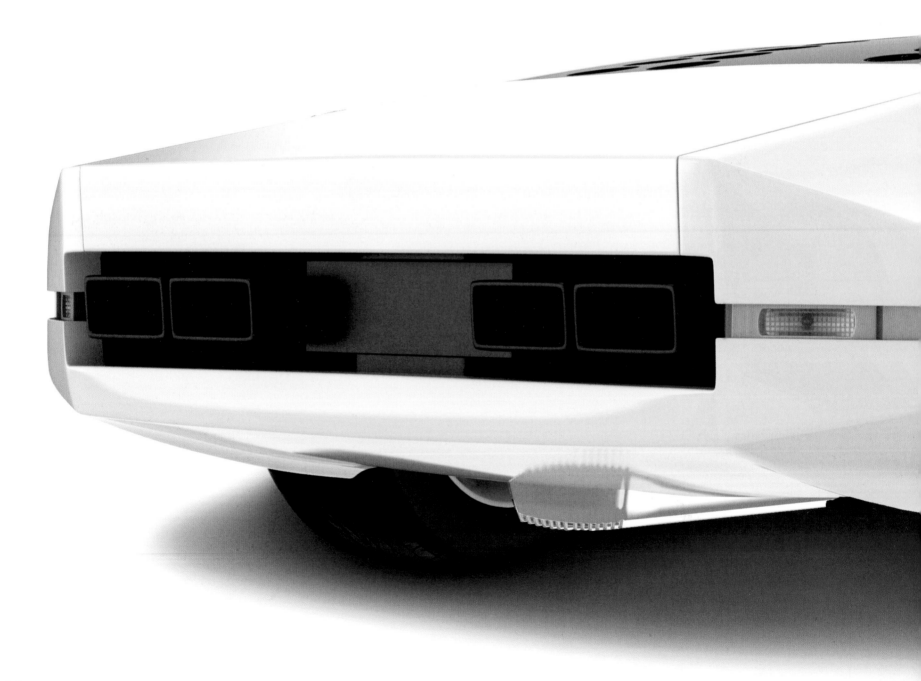

Clutch:	Multi-plate
Gearbox:	Manual, 5-speed + reverse

CHASSIS

Bodywork:	Two-seater berlinetta
Frame:	Tubular steel
Front suspension:	Independent, unequal-length wishbones, coil springs, telescopic shock absorbers, anti-roll bar
Rear suspension:	Independent, unequal-length wishbones, coil springs, telescopic shock absorbers, anti-roll bar
Steering:	Rack and pinion
Front/rear brakes:	Disc
Wheels:	15-in alloy rims with 11.5 x 15 (front) and 14.5 x 15 (rear) tires

DIMENSIONS AND WEIGHT

Wheelbase:	94.5 in (2,400 mm)
Front/rear track:	59.8/59.5 in (1,518/1,511 mm)
Length:	176.4 in (4,480 mm)
Width:	80.6 in (2,048 mm)
Height:	32.8 in (834 mm)
Weight:	—
Fuel tank capacity:	32 gal (120 liters)

PERFORMANCE

Top speed:	—
Acceleration 0 to 60 mph (0 to 100 km/h):	—
Weight/power ratio:	—

FERRARI 365 GTB/4 DAYTONA

1968

This successor to the 275 GTB/4 became known as the "Daytona" in recognition of the 1-2-3 victory of the Ferrari 330 P4 in the 24 Hours of Daytona race in 1967. Designed by Pininfarina, it had a revolutionary, very aerodynamic style and was tasked with a mission that was anything but easy—combating the rival Lamborghini Miura on the grand touring market. Ferrari used the best technology available at the time. The front-mounted 269 cu in (4.4 liter) V12 delivered 352 hp and had twin overhead camshafts for each bank. The transaxle transmission of the 275 GTB/4 was adopted, with the gearbox being mounted together with the differential on the back axle rather than at the front with the engine, as had been the case in the past.

The first series had the fixed-headlight assembly mounted behind a full-width plexiglass strip. This arrangement was replaced in 1971 by the more-conventional retractable units.

Other special features included the sports seats and the inside panels of the doors. These were upholstered with perforated leather lozenges stitched crossways—a finishing touch destined to become part of the Ferrari style icon. A spider version, the GTS/4, destined for the U.S. market, was introduced in 1969. This was the last 12-cylinder supercar to be officially imported into the USA and the last to be announced before Fiat took over control of road-car production at Maranello.

TECHNICAL DATA

ENGINE

Type:	Front, longitudinal
Cylinders:	V12 (60°)
Bore x stroke:	3.19 x 2.80 in (81.0 x 71.0 mm)
Displacement:	268 cu in (4,390 cc)
Maximum power:	352 hp at 7,500 rpm
Maximum torque:	318 lb-ft (44.0 kgm) at 5,500 rpm
Valve actuation:	Twin overhead camshafts per bank
Valves:	Two per cylinder
Fuel feed:	Six Weber 40 DCN/20 carburetors

Ignition:	One spark plug per cylinder, twin coils
Cooling:	Water-cooled
Lubrication:	Dry sump

TRANSMISSION

Drive:	Rear-wheel drive
Clutch:	Dry single-plate
Gearbox:	Manual, 5-speed + reverse

CHASSIS

Bodywork:	Two-seater berlinetta
Frame:	Tubular steel trellis

Front suspension:	Independent, double wishbones, coil springs, telescopic shock absorbers, anti-roll bar
Rear suspension:	Independent, double wishbones, coil springs, telescopic shock absorbers, anti-roll bar
Steering:	Worm and roller
Front/rear brakes:	Disc
Wheels:	15-in light alloy rims with 215/70 tires front and rear

DIMENSIONS AND WEIGHT

| Wheelbase: | 94.5 in (2,400 mm) |

Front/rear track:	56.7/57.2 in (1,440/1,453 mm)
Length:	174.2 in (4,425 mm)
Width:	69.3 in (1,760 mm)
Height:	49.0 in (1,245 mm)
Weight:	2,646 lb (1,200 kg)
Fuel tank capacity:	34 gal (128 liters)

PERFORMANCE

Top speed:	174 mph (280 km/h)
Acceleration 0 to 60 mph (0 to 100 km/h):	5.4 seconds
Weight/power ratio:	7.52 lb/hp (3.41 kg/hp)

FERRARI DINO 246 GT

1969

The successor to the 206 GT, this was the first road-going Ferrari to have the Dino name. It was the result of a joint project between Ferrari and Fiat and revived the name of a single-seater Formula 1 Ferrari from the end of the nineteen-fifties.

Dino was the diminutive of Alfredo, Enzo Ferrari's son who had taken part in the design of a 6-cylinder engine. Dino died in 1956, and the car was named in his memory. Not surprisingly, the car had a transverse, central V6, taken from the 206 GT and uprated from 122 to 147 cu in (2 to 2.4 liters).

The upgrade was necessary to compensate for the increase in weight from 1,984 lb to 2,381 lb (900 to 1,080 kg) when the aluminum bodywork was abandoned in favor of a steel one. Only the doors, hood, and trunk remained in aluminum. The 147 cu in (2,419 cc) V6 delivered 195 hp and was later to be adopted on the celebrated Lancia Stratos. There were some differences compared to the 206 GT. The wheelbase and overall length were longer by 2.4 in and 3.4 in (6 cm and 8.5 cm) respectively. The fuel filler cap was no longer outside but was now hidden under a flush-fitting flap.

The alloy wheels had five lug nuts instead of the central wing nuts. Designed by Pininfarina, the 246 GT was thought of as the baby Ferrari. Like the Dino 206 GT, it heralded the introduction of a change in the way of identifying Maranello cars. After the zeroes had been removed, the first two numbers indicated the displacement and the last number indicated the number of cylinders. In the past, the last number had indicated the unitary displacement.

Three series of this car were produced in both berlinetta (the GT) and targa (the GTS from 1972) versions.

TECHNICAL DATA

ENGINE

Type:	Central, transverse
Cylinders:	V6 (65°)
Bore x stroke:	3.64 x 2.36 in (92.5 x 60.0 mm)
Displacement:	148 cu in (2,419 cc)
Maximum power:	195 hp at 7,600 rpm
Maximum torque:	166 lb-ft (23.0 kgm) at 5,500 rpm
Valve actuation:	Twin overhead camshafts per bank
Valves:	Two per cylinder
Fuel feed:	Three Weber 40 DCN F/1-F/7 carburetors
Ignition:	One spark plug per cylinder, single coil
Cooling:	Water-cooled
Lubrication:	Wet sump

TRANSMISSION

Drive:	Rear-wheel drive

Clutch:	Dry single plate
Gearbox:	Manual, 5-speed + reverse

CHASSIS

Bodywork:	Two-seater berlinetta
Frame:	Tubular steel trellis
Front suspension:	Independent, unequal-length wishbones, coil springs, telescopic shock absorbers, anti-roll bar
Rear suspension:	Independent, unequal-length wishbones, coil springs, telescopic shock absorbers, anti-roll bar
Steering:	Rack and pinion
Front/rear brakes:	Disc
Wheels:	14-in light alloy rims with 205/70 tires front & rear

DIMENSIONS AND WEIGHT

Wheelbase:	92.1 in (2,340 mm)
Front/rear track:	56.1/56.3 in (1,425/1,430 mm)
Length:	166.7 in (4,235 mm)
Width:	66.9 in (1,700 mm)
Height:	44.7 in (1,135 mm)
Weight:	2,381 lb (1,080 kg)
Fuel tank capacity:	17 gal (65 liters)

PERFORMANCE

Top speed:	152 mph (245 km/h)
Acceleration 0 to 60 mph (0 to 100 km/h):	7.3 seconds
Weight/power ratio:	12.21 lb/hp (5.54 kg/hp)

FERRARI 365
GT/4 BB

1971

TECHNICAL DATA

ENGINE

Type:	Central, longitudinal
Cylinders:	V12 (180°)
Bore x stroke:	3.19 x 2.80 in (81.0 x 71.0 mm)
Displacement:	268 cu in (4,390 cc)
Maximum power:	380 hp at 7,700 rpm
Maximum torque:	318 lb-ft (44.0 kgm) at 4,000 rpm
Valve actuation:	Twin overhead camshafts per bank
Valves:	Two per cylinder
Fuel feed:	Four Weber 40 IF3C carburetors
Ignition:	One spark plug per cylinder, single coil
Cooling:	Water-cooled
Lubrication:	Wet sump

TRANSMISSION

Drive:	Rear-wheel drive
Clutch:	Dry single-plate
Gearbox:	Manual, 5-speed + reverse

CHASSIS

Bodywork:	Two-seater berlinetta

Frame:	Tubular steel trellis
Front suspension:	Independent, double wishbones, coil springs, telescopic shock absorbers, anti-roll bar
Rear suspension:	Independent, double wishbones, coil springs, telescopic shock absorbers, anti-roll bar
Steering:	Rack and pinion
Front/rear brakes :	Disc
Wheels:	15-in light alloy rims with 215/70 tires front & rear

DIMENSIONS AND WEIGHT

Wheelbase:	98.4 in (2,500 mm)
Front/rear track:	59.1/59.1 in (1,500/1,500 mm)
Length:	171.7 in (4,360 mm)
Width:	70.9 in (1,800 mm)
Height:	44.1 in (1,120 mm)
Weight:	2,557 lb (1,160 kg)
Fuel tank capacity:	32 gal (120 liters)

PERFORMANCE

Top speed:	186 mph (300 km/h)
Acceleration 0 to 60 mph (0 to 100 km/h):	5.3 seconds
Weight/power ratio:	6.72 lb/hp (3.05 kg/hp)

The GT/4 BB marked a true break with tradition at Ferrari. The 12-cylinder V architecture traditionally employed at Maranello gave way to a flat boxer configuration. The engine was now mid-mounted, ending the long tradition of front-mounted power units on Ferrari grand touring cars. The flat-12 had already been tried on the 250 LM, a car which for all practical purposes was a competition vehicle adapted for road use.

The model title followed standard Ferrari practice, with the number 365 referring to the unitary displacement, the number 4 relating to the total number of camshafts and the suffix "BB" standing for "Berlinetta Boxer." Despite the name, the engine was not a boxer in the true sense of the word. The cylinders were arranged in a 180° flat V, a layout used by Ferrari at that time for its competition engines. The two-tone bodywork had the lower part painted satin black and featured retractable headlights. The frame followed the classic Ferrari principle of a tubular steel chassis frame joined to substructures. Here there was another innovation, too: the steel panels of the cabin became an integral part of the structure, to form a rigid central cell. Presented in 1971, it did not go into production until 1973, probably so as not to undermine the success of the 365 GTB/4 Daytona whose popularity showed no signs of waning.

Another époque-making change for the Prancing Horse marque. Maranello's smaller vehicles had previously sported the Dino name, but were now to carry the Ferrari badge. The change was dictated by the oil crisis and also the need to win over new market segments. The 308 GTB was the successor to the less commercially fortunate Dino 208 and 308 GT4 designed by Bertone.

It borrowed the transversely mid-mounted 90° V8 engine of the 308 GT4, but this time with dry-sump lubrication in place of the wet sump of its predecessor and a rated power output of 255 hp. The engine had two valves per cylinder and was fed by four Weber carburetors. In 1980, Bosch K-Jetronic fuel injection was fitted and the model name was changed accordingly to GTBi. Power output dropped from 255 to 214 hp. In 1982, the Quattrovalvole (QV) version was introduced. As the name suggests, this had four valves per cylinder. Designed by Pininfarina and considered to be the true successor to the much-prized Dino 246 GT, the 308 GTB/GTS originally had a fiberglass body, replaced in 1977 by an all-steel body. The 5-speed gearbox was coupled in a unit with the engine. The car was extraordinarily successful and remained in production until 1985. A targa-topped version, the GTS, was introduced in 1977 and rapidly shot to stardom as the "official" car of the actor Tom Selleck in the successful TV series *Magnum P.I.*

FERRARI 308 GTB/GTS

1975

TECHNICAL DATA

ENGINE

Type:	Central, transverse
Cylinders:	V8 (90°)
Bore x stroke:	3.19 x 2.80 in (81.0 x 71.0 mm)
Displacement:	179 cu in (2,927 cc)
Maximum power:	255 hp at 7,700 rpm (GTBi/GTSi 214 hp, QV 240 hp)
Maximum torque:	–
Valve actuation:	Twin overhead camshafts per bank
Valves:	Two per cylinder (QV four per cylinder)
Fuel feed:	Four Weber 40 DCNF carburetors (GTBi/GTSi and QV Bosch K-Jetronic fuel injection)
Ignition:	One spark plug per cylinder, single coil
Cooling:	Water-cooled
Lubrication:	Dry sump

TRANSMISSION

Drive:	Rear-wheel drive
Clutch:	Dry single-plate
Gearbox:	Manual, 5-speed + reverse

CHASSIS

Bodywork:	Two-seater berlinetta/spider
Frame:	Tubular steel trellis
Front suspension:	Independent, double wishbones, coil springs, telescopic shock absorbers, anti-roll bar
Rear suspension:	Independent, double wishbones, coil springs, telescopic shock absorbers, anti-roll bar
Steering:	Rack and pinion
Front/rear brakes :	Disc
Wheels:	14-in light alloy rims with 205/70 tires front and rear

DIMENSIONS AND WEIGHT

Wheelbase:	92.1 in (2,340 mm)
Front/rear track:	57.5/57.5 in (1,460/1,460 mm)
Length:	166.5 in (4,230 mm)
Width:	67.7 in (1,720 mm)
Height:	44.1 in (1,120 mm)
Weight:	2,403 lb/1,090 kg (fiberglass bodywork); 2,646 lb/1,200 kg (steel bodywork)
Fuel tank capacity:	21 gal/80 liters (GTBi/GTSi - QV 20 gal/74 liters)

PERFORMANCE

Top speed:	157 mph or 252 km/h (GTBi/GTSi 149 mph or 240 km/h, QV 158 mph or 255 km/h)
Acceleration 0 to 60 mph (0 to 100 km/h):	–
Weight/power ratio:	4.27 kg/hp (GTB with fiberglass bodywork)

FERRARI 288 GTO

1984

A name with an illustrious history, GTO stands for Gran Turismo Omologato (literally "homologated grand tourer") and recalls the 250 GTO berlinetta of 1962, one of the most victorious and attractive Ferraris ever built. Derived from the 308 GTB and designed by Pininfarina, the 288 GTO was expressly designed for participation in competitions for Group B vehicles. However, a change in regulations put an immediate end to the car's competition career, and it was converted to road use.

Outwardly, it resembled the 308 but with a more muscular look, with bulbous front and rear quarterpanels, a lower stance, and bigger spoilers. Technically, however, there were fundamental differences. The wheelbase was longer (96.5 in/2,450 mm compared to 92.1 in/2,340 mm), and the mid V8 was longitudinally rather than transversely mounted. Electronic fuel injection replaced carburetors. The bodywork was made from composite material rather than the fiberglass/steel used on the 308.

The 90° V8 was the first Ferrari power unit to be turbocharged with twin turbochargers assisted by a pair of intercoolers. Despite the relatively low 171 cu in (2.8 liter) capacity, the engine developed a massive (for that time) 400 hp and provided performance worthy of any race car. The GTO (the 288 prefix was used mainly to distinguish this model from its predecessor the 250) became one of the most sought-after models for collectors. Two hundred and seventy-two examples were built—72 more than planned.

TECHNICAL DATA

ENGINE

Type:	Central, longitudinal
Cylinders:	V8 (90°)
Bore x stroke:	3.15 x 2.80 in (80.0 x 71.0 mm)
Displacement:	174 cu in (2,855 cc)
Maximum power:	400 hp at 7,000 rpm
Maximum torque:	366 lb-ft (50.6 kgm) at 3,800 rpm
Valve actuation:	Twin overhead camshafts per bank
Valves:	Four per cylinder
Fuel feed:	Weber-Marelli electronic fuel injection, twin IHI turbochargers, two intercoolers

Ignition:	One spark plug per cylinder, Weber-Marelli electronic
Cooling:	Water-cooled
Lubrication:	Dry sump

TRANSMISSION

Drive:	Rear-wheel drive
Clutch:	Twin-plate
Gearbox:	Manual, 5-speed + reverse

CHASSIS

Bodywork:	Two-seater berlinetta
Frame:	Tubular steel trellis

Front suspension:	Independent, double wishbones, coil springs, telescopic shock absorbers, anti-roll bar		Width:	75.2 in (1,910 mm)
			Height:	44.1 in (1,120 mm)
Rear suspension:	Independent, double wishbones, coil springs, telescopic shock absorbers, anti-roll bar		Weight:	45.7 in (1,160 kg)
			Fuel tank capacity:	32 gal (120 liters)
Steering:	Rack and pinion			
Front/rear brakes :	Ventilated discs			
Wheels:	16-in magnesium alloy rims with 225/55 (front) and 265/50 (rear) tires			

PERFORMANCE

Top speed:	190 mph (305 km/h)
Acceleration 0 to 60 mph (0 to 100 km/h):	4.9 seconds
Weight/power ratio:	6.39 lb/hp (2.90 kg/hp)

DIMENSIONS AND WEIGHT

Wheelbase:	96.5 in (2,450 mm)
Front/rear track:	61.4/61.5 in (1,559/1,562 mm)
Length:	168.9 in (4,290 mm)

FERRARI TESTAROSSA

1984

This was a golden year for Ferrari. It saw the return of the GTO and the introduction of another new car bearing a name famous in the annals of Ferrari: Testa Rossa. The name was originally given to the 1956 500 TR barchetta, and then later to the 1957 250 spider. The name Testa Rossa is Italian for "red head" and refers to the paint color of the camshaft covers. During the nineteen-eighties, the name became one word: Testarossa. Designed by Pininfarina, this radically different supercar from the Prancing Horse marque broke all the design rules of the time. This successor to the 512 BBi had deeply straked door panels where the door louvers fed cooling air to the side-mounted radiators. The rectangular combination light units at

the rear were hidden behind a full-width, horizontally slatted satin black louvre. Another original feature was the single exterior mirror mounted on the driver's-side windshield pillar. Later, in 1987, this was abandoned in favor of a more conventional setup. The rear track was considerably wider than the front track (65.4 in/1,660 mm compared to 59.8 in/1,518 mm). The bodywork was mainly aluminum. The power unit was a 302 cu in (4,943 cc) 180° V12 delivering 390 hp with twin overhead camshafts per bank and four valves per cylinder. The 1984 Testarossa remained in production until 1991, when it was replaced by the 512 TR. A single spider example was built by Pininfarina in 1985 for the personal use of Fiat supremo Gianni Agnelli.

TECHNICAL DATA

ENGINE

Type:	Central, longitudinal
Cylinders:	V12 (180°)
Bore x stroke:	3.23 x 3.07 in (82.0 x 78.0 mm)
Displacement:	302 cu in (4,943 cc)
Maximum power:	390 hp at 6,300 rpm
Maximum torque:	362 lb-ft (50.0 kgm) at 4,500 rpm
Valve actuation:	Twin overhead camshafts per bank
Valves:	Four per cylinder
Fuel feed:	Bosch K-Jetronic fuel injection
Ignition:	Marelli Microplex electronic, one spark plug per cylinder
Cooling:	Water-cooled
Lubrication:	Dry sump

TRANSMISSION

Drive:	Rear-wheel drive
Clutch:	Twin-plate
Gearbox:	Manual, 5-speed + reverse

CHASSIS

Bodywork:	Two-seater berlinetta
Frame:	Tubular steel trellis
Front suspension:	Independent, double wishbones, coil springs, twin telescopic shock absorbers, anti-roll bar
Rear suspension:	Independent, double wishbones, coil springs, twin telescopic shock absorbers, anti-roll bar
Steering:	Rack and pinion
Front/rear brakes :	Ventilated discs
Wheels:	16-in light alloy rims with 225/50 (front) and 255/50 (rear) tires

DIMENSIONS AND WEIGHT

Wheelbase:	100.4 in (2,550 mm)
Front/rear track:	59.8/65.4 in (1,518/1,660 mm)
Length:	176.6 in (4,485 mm)
Width:	77.8 in (1,976 mm)
Height:	44.5 in (1,130 mm)
Weight:	3,320 lb (1,506 kg)
Fuel tank capacity:	32 gal (120 liters)

PERFORMANCE

Top speed:	180 mph (290 km/h)
Acceleration 0 to 60 mph (0 to 100 km/h):	5.8 seconds
Weight/power ratio:	8.51 lb/hp (3.86 kg/hp)

FERRARI 328 GTB

1985

This was the natural evolution of the 308 GTB/GTS series, but with greatly improved mechanics. The 328 GTB had the same transverse, centrally mounted V8 as its 1975 predecessor, but with the displacement increased from 179 to 194 cu in (2,927 to 3,186 cc). The valve train had the same twin overhead camshafts and four valves per cylinder as the "old" 308 Quattrovalvole.

Electronic ignition replaced coil ignition. The maximum power output was increased from 240 hp for the 308 QV to 270 hp, result-

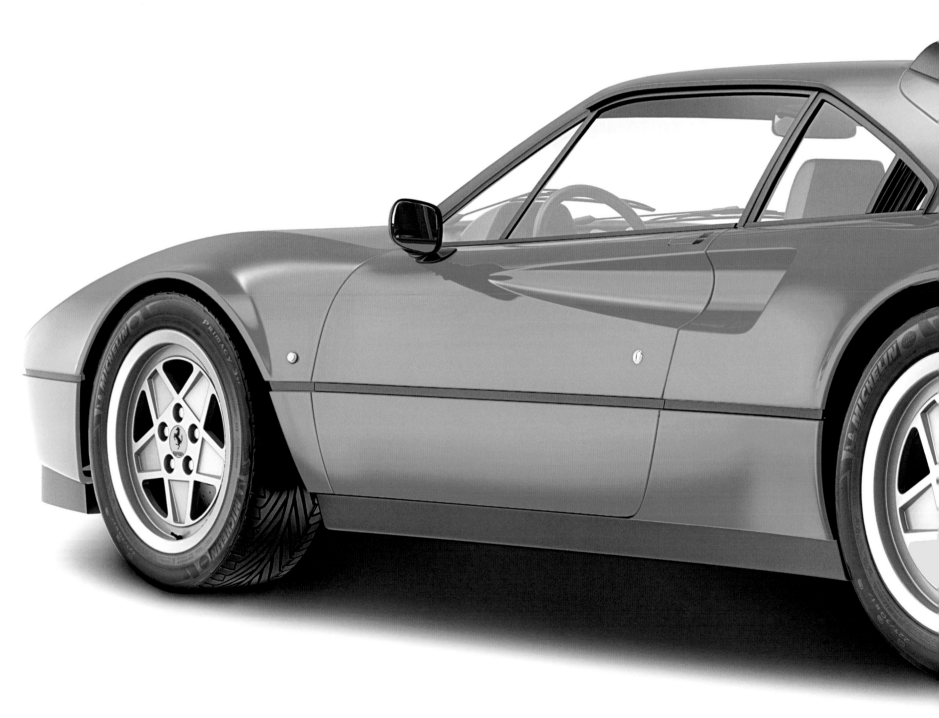

ing in a top speed of 163 mph (263 km/h) and a 0-to-60-mph (0-to-100-km/h) time of 6.4 seconds.

The 328 figures in the model name referred to the total displacement of the engine, 3.2 liters (195 cu in), and 8 for the number of cylinders. GTB stood for Gran Turismo Berlinetta. Designed by Pininfarina, the car had body-color bumpers, and the bodywork had a softer, more rounded styling than the 308 GTB. This reflected the work done for the Mondial 3.2 models, with which the 328 GTB shared a similar radiator grille and front-light assembly layout. In the middle of 1988, the brakes could be fitted with the antilock braking system (ABS). Like the 308 series, the 5-speed manual gearbox was coupled in unit with the engine.

The 328 GTB remained in production for four years, until it was replaced in 1989 by the 348 TB. Commercially, the GTB was not a resounding success, only 1,500 cars being sold. The 308 GTS spider, in comparison, sold over 6,000 units.

TECHNICAL DATA

ENGINE

Type:	Central, transverse
Cylinders:	V8 (90°)
Bore x stroke:	3.27 x 2.90 in (83.0 x 73.6 mm)
Displacement:	194 cu in (3,186 cc)
Maximum power:	270 hp at 7,000 rpm
Maximum torque:	224 lb-ft (31.0 kgm) at 5,500 rpm
Valve actuation:	Twin overhead camshafts per bank
Valves:	Four per cylinder
Fuel feed:	Bosch K-Jetronic fuel injection

Ignition:	Marelli Microplex electronic, one spark plug per cylinder
Cooling:	Water-cooled
Lubrication:	Wet sump

TRANSMISSION

Drive:	Rear-wheel drive
Clutch:	Dry single-plate
Gearbox:	Manual, 5-speed + reverse

CHASSIS

Bodywork:	Two-seater berlinetta

Frame:	Tubular steel trellis
Front suspension:	Independent, double wishbones, coil springs, telescopic shock absorbers, anti-roll bar
Rear suspension:	Independent, double wishbones, coil springs, telescopic shock absorbers, anti-roll bar
Steering:	Rack and pinion
Front/rear brakes :	Disc
Wheels:	16-in light alloy rims with 205/55 (front) and 225/50 (rear) tires

DIMENSIONS AND WEIGHT

Wheelbase:	92.5 in (2,350 mm)
Front/rear track:	58.5/57.7 in (1,485/1,465 mm)
Length:	167.5 in (4,255 mm)
Width:	68.1 in (1,730 mm)
Height:	44.4 in (1,128 mm)
Weight:	2,784 lb (1,263 kg)
Fuel tank capacity:	20 gal (74 liters)

PERFORMANCE

Top speed:	163 mph (263 km/h)
Acceleration 0 to 60 mph (0 to 100 km/h)	6.4 seconds
Weight/power ratio:	10.32 lb/hp (4.68 kg/hp)

FERRARI 412

1985

The 412 was the first Ferrari to offer Bosch ABS as standard equipment. The 412 was the successor to the 2+2 400i, which in turn had taken the place of the historic 365 GT4 2+2 of 1972. It was powered by a front-mounted 302 cu in (4,943 cc) V12 producing 340 hp. It was available either with a 5-speed manual gearbox or a 3-speed automatic transmission with a General Motors torque-converter unit, which had made its debut on the 400i. Designed by Pininfarina, this

spacious 2+2 with the Prancing Horse badge had Marelli Microplex electronic ignition. The bumpers were body-color-coded, and standard equipment included items otherwise considered to be luxury options at the time: leather interiors, power-assisted steering, air conditioning, radio, and central door locks. Enzo Ferrari personally gave a 412 to Michele Alboreto on the birth of the Ferrari driver's first child. The 412 model designation referred to the swept volume of a single cylinder. The car remained in production until 1989. This brought to an end a seventeen-year run of what was essentially a single body style, given the close family likeness between the 412, the 365 GT4 2+2, and the 400i, a record. We would have to wait until 1992 for the 456GT before a 2+2 model reappeared in the Ferrari catalog, and it would be nearly seven years before automatic transmissions would once again become available on a Ferrari.

TECHNICAL DATA

ENGINE

Type:	Front, longitudinal
Cylinders:	V12 (60°)
Bore x stroke:	3.23 x 3.07 in (82.0 x 78.0 mm)
Displacement:	302 cu in (4,943 cc)
Maximum power:	340 hp at 6,000 rpm
Maximum torque:	333 lb-ft (46.0 kgm) at 4,200 rpm
Valve actuation:	Twin overhead camshafts per bank
Valves:	Two per cylinder
Fuel feed:	Bosch K-Jetronic fuel injection

Ignition:	Marelli Microplex electronic, one spark plug per cylinder
Cooling:	Water-cooled
Lubrication:	Wet sump

TRANSMISSION

Drive:	Rear-wheel drive
Clutch:	Dry twin-plate (manual)/Torque converter (automatic)
Gearbox:	Manual, 5-speed + reverse/Automatic, 3-speed + reverse

CHASSIS

Bodywork:	2+2 coupé

Frame:	Tubular steel trellis
Front suspension:	Independent, double wishbones, coil springs, telescopic shock absorbers, anti-roll bar
Rear suspension:	Independent, double wishbones, coil springs, telescopic shock absorbers, anti-roll bar
Steering:	Rack and pinion
Front/rear brakes :	Disc
Wheels:	16-in light alloy rims with 240/55 tires front and rear

DIMENSIONS AND WEIGHT

Wheelbase:	106.3 in (2,700 mm)

Front/rear track:	58.3/59.1 in (1,480/1,500 mm)
Length:	189.4 in (4,810 mm)
Width:	70.8 in (1,798 mm)
Height:	51.7 in (1,314 mm)
Weight:	3,979 lb/3,990 lb (1,805 kg/1,810 kg) (automatic)
Fuel tank capacity:	32 gal (120 liters)

PERFORMANCE

Top speed:	152/158 mph (245/255 km/h) (automatic)
Acceleration 0 to 60 mph (0 to 100 km/h):	6.7 seconds/8.3 seconds (automatic)
Weight/power ratio:	11.71/11.73 lb/hp (5.31/5.32 kg/hp) (automatic)

FERRARI F40

1987

The F40 was a racecar adapted for road use, but also a supercar built to celebrate Ferrari's 40th anniversary as a car maker. The car was a sensation, enjoying a success that exceeded all expectations. Demand was such that Ferrari was "obliged" to make over 1,300 units, rather than the 400 originally planned. This car was the spiritual successor to the 288 GTO. Designed by Pininfarina, it had a raw, mean look that faithfully portrayed its true character. Powered by a 177 cu

in (2.9 liter), 32-valve V8 producing 478 hp, the engine had twin turbo-chargers feeding intake air via a pair of intercoolers at 16 psi (1.1 bar) to produce a terrifying 2.67 hp/cu in (162.8 hp/liter). The wheelbase was identical to the 288 GTO (96.5 in/2,450 mm), but the tubular steel chassis frame had composite inserts that provided greatly superior rigidity. This was the first series car to be fitted with Kevlar and fiberglass bodywork. The cross-drilled ventilated disc brakes were not power-assisted. A height-adjustable electronically controlled suspension system became available during the production period. The interior was as spartan as any competition car, with the air-conditioning being the only concession to comfort. There were no electric windows, and the first examples had plexiglass panels instead of glass for the side windows and rear window. It remained in production until 1992 and was followed by the F50.

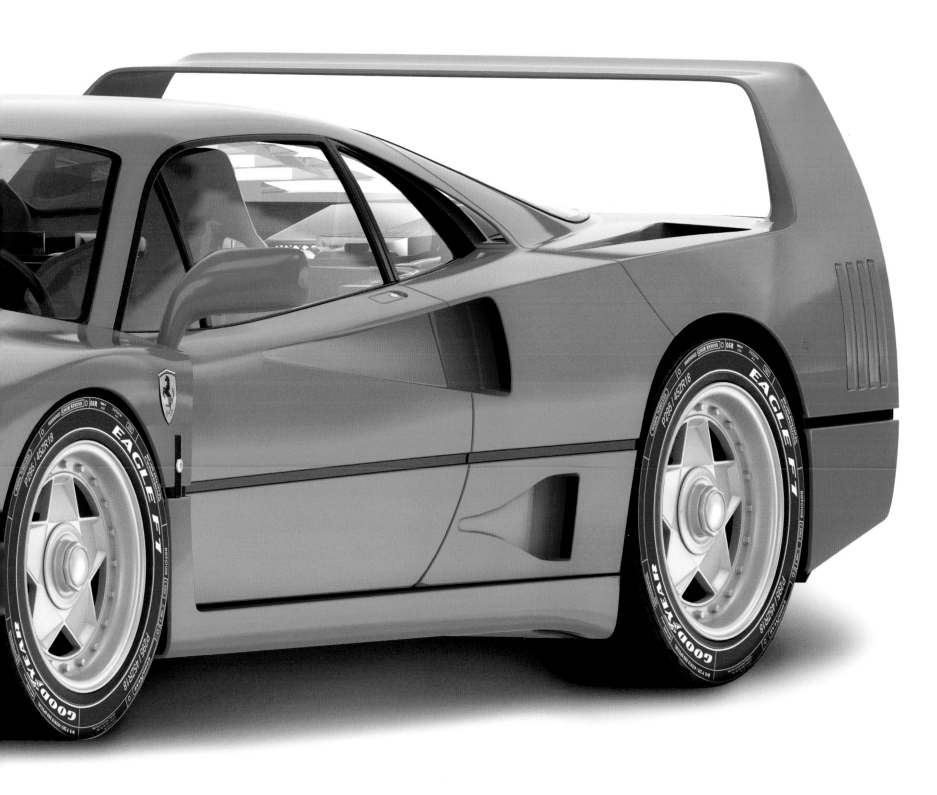

TECHNICAL DATA

ENGINE

Type:	Central, longitudinal
Cylinders:	V8 (90°)
Bore x stroke:	3.23 x 2.74 in (82.0 x 69.5 mm)
Displacement:	179 cu in (2,936 cc)
Maximum power:	478 hp at 7,000 rpm
Maximum torque:	426 lb-ft (58.9 kgm) at 4,000 rpm
Valve actuation:	Twin overhead camshafts per bank
Valves:	Four per cylinder
Fuel feed:	Weber-Marelli electronic fuel injection, twin IHI turbochargers, two intercoolers

Ignition:	One spark plug per cylinder, Weber-Marelli electronic
Cooling:	Water-cooled
Lubrication:	Dry sump

TRANSMISSION

Drive:	Rear-wheel drive
Clutch:	Twin-plate
Gearbox:	Manual, 5-speed + reverse

CHASSIS

Bodywork:	Two-seater berlinetta
Frame:	Tubular steel with composite components

Front suspension:	Independent, double wishbones, coil springs, telescopic shock absorbers, anti-roll bar
Rear suspension:	Independent, double wishbones, coil springs, telescopic shock absorbers, anti-roll bar
Steering:	Rack and pinion
Front/rear brakes :	Cross-drilled, ventilated discs
Wheels:	17-in light alloy rims with 245/40 (front) and 335/35 (rear) tires

DIMENSIONS AND WEIGHT

Wheelbase:	96.5 in (2,450 mm)
Front/rear track:	62.8/63.2 in (1,594/1,606 mm)

Length:	171.6 in (4,358 mm)
Width:	77.6 in (1,970 mm)
Height:	44.3 in (1,124 mm)
Weight:	2,425 lb (1,100 kg)
Fuel tank capacity:	32 gal (120 liters)

PERFORMANCE

Top speed:	201 mph (324 km/h)
Acceleration 0 to 60 mph (0 to 100 km/h):	4.1 seconds
Weight/power ratio:	5.07 lb/hp (2.30 kg/hp)

FERRARI 512 TR

1991

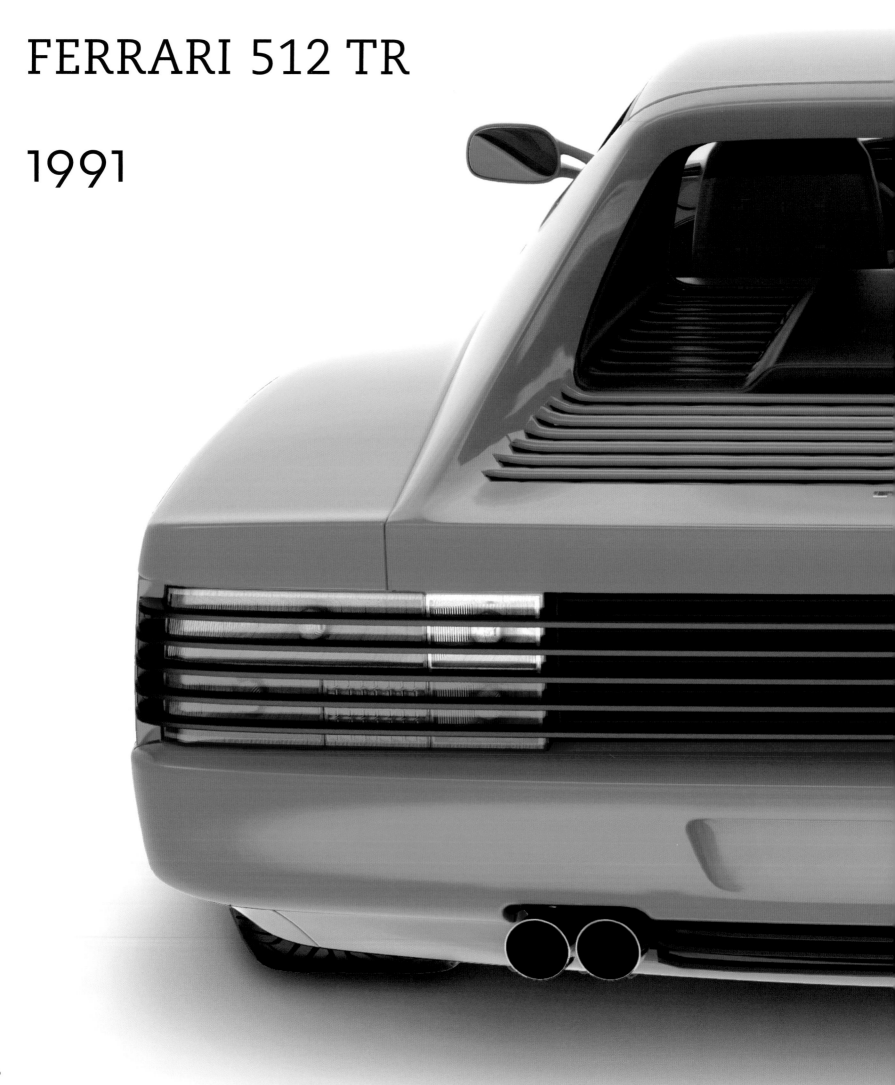

An evolution of the 1984 Testarossa, the new car also marked a return to the model identification system using characters. The figure 5 referred to the displacement of the engine in liters and the 12 to the number of cylinders, while the TR was an abbreviation of Testa Rossa. The differences in styling were relatively few and concentrated mainly on a new front grille and five-spoke grooved alloy road wheels with an innovative star design. There were radical changes to the interiors, which were now much more comfortable and ergonomic.

The 180° V12 had the same displacement as before, 302 cu in (4,943 cc). Changes to the intake system, larger valves, re-profiled camshafts, and the Bosch Motronic M2.7 electronic ignition and fuel injection system contributed to raising the maximum power output from 390 to 428 hp. Performance was improved with special pistons that raised the compression ratio from 9.3:1 to 10.0:1. In addition, the engine-and-transmission assembly location was dropped by 30mm to lower the center of gravity, thus improving the responsiveness and roadholding of this Testarossa.

The wheelbase remained the same as before at 100.4 in (2,550 mm). The braking system could be fitted with ABS, and the weight of the vehicle dropped by about 73 lb (33 kg), from 3,320 lb to 3,247 lb (1,506 to 1,473 kg). The 512 TR remained in production until 1994, when the F512 M, a further development of the TR theme, took its place.

TECHNICAL DATA

ENGINE

Type:	Central, longitudinal
Cylinders:	V12 (180°)
Bore x stroke:	3.23 x 3.07 in (82.0 x 78.0 mm)
Displacement:	302 cu in (4,943 cc)
Maximum power:	428 hp at 6,750 rpm
Maximum torque:	362 lb-ft (50.1 kgm) at 5,500 rpm
Valve actuation:	Twin overhead camshafts per bank
Valves:	Four per cylinder
Fuel feed:	Bosch Motronic M2.7 electronic fuel injection
Ignition:	Bosch Motronic M2.7 electronic, single spark plug per cylinder
Cooling:	Water-cooled
Lubrication:	Dry sump

TRANSMISSION

Drive:	Rear-wheel drive
Clutch:	Dry single-plate
Gearbox:	Manual, 5-speed + reverse

CHASSIS

Bodywork:	Two-seater berlinetta
Frame:	Tubular steel trellis
Front suspension:	Independent, double wishbones, coil springs, twin telescopic shock absorbers, anti-roll bar
Rear suspension:	Independent, double wishbones, coil springs, twin telescopic shock absorbers, anti-roll bar
Steering:	Rack and pinion
Front/rear brakes :	Ventilated discs
Wheels:	18-in light alloy rims with 235/40 (front) and 295/35 (rear) tires

DIMENSIONS AND WEIGHT

Wheelbase:	100.4 in (2,550 mm)
Front/rear track:	60.3/64.7 in (1,532/1,644 mm)
Length:	176.4 in (4,480 mm)
Width:	77.8 in (1,976 mm)
Height:	44.7 in (1,135 mm)
Weight:	3,247 lb (1,473 kg)
Fuel tank capacity:	26 gal (100 liters)

PERFORMANCE

Top speed:	195 mph (314 km/h)
Acceleration 0 to 60 (mph 0 to 100 km/h):	4.8 seconds
Weight/power ratio:	7.58 lb/hp (3.44 kg/hp)

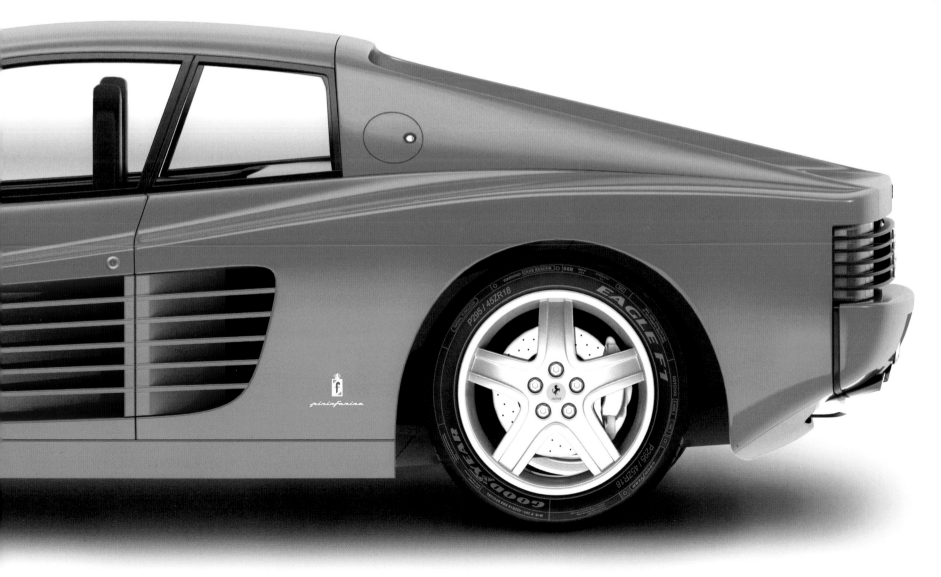

FERRARI F355 BERLINETTA

1994

Another turning point. The debut of the F1-style electro-hydraulic gearbox-management system operated by paddles on the steering wheel. This futuristic solution, originally developed for race cars, was now fitted for the first time on a road car. The name of the F355 indicated that it had a total displacement of 214 cu in (3.5 liters) and 5 valves per cylinder.

Designed by Pininfarina, the F355 was powered by a mid-rear 90° V8 mounted longitudinally, and featured titanium con-rods and twin

overhead camshafts on each bank. An innovative break with the past came with the fitting of 5 valves per cylinder, rather than the 4-valve configuration widely used at the time. The V8 delivered 380 hp and was mounted together with the gearbox on a tubular steel trellis sub-frame. The main chassis-frame structure was a steel monocoque, another innovative solution for the time. The suspension was electronically controlled and had two settings which could be selected from the cabin.

The aerodynamics of the aluminum-and-steel bodywork received particular attention, and the very clean aerodynamic design was extended to include a full-body undertray designed to increase downforce. Initially the car was fitted with the conventional manual 6-speed gearbox. In 1997, as said, it was introduced the electro-hydraulic gearbox-management system originally developed for Ferrari's Formula 1 cars. Available also in GTS (targa-top) and spider versions, the F355 was replaced by the 360 Modena in 1999.

TECHNICAL DATA

ENGINE

Type:	Central, longitudinal
Cylinders:	V8 (90°)
Bore x stroke:	3.35 x 3.03 in (85.0 x 77.0 mm)
Displacement:	213 cu in (3,496 cc)
Maximum power:	380 hp at 8,250 rpm
Maximum torque:	268 lb-ft (37.0 kgm) at 6,000 rpm
Valve actuation:	Twin overhead camshafts per bank
Valves:	Five per cylinder
Fuel feed:	Bosch Motronic M2.7 electronic fuel injection

Ignition:	Bosch Motronic M2.7 static electronic, single spark plug per cylinder
Cooling:	Water-cooled
Lubrication:	Dry sump

TRANSMISSION

Drive:	Rear-wheel drive
Clutch:	Dry single-plate
Gearbox:	Manual, 6-speed + reverse (also with F1 electro-hydraulic 6-speed + reverse from 1997)

CHASSIS

Bodywork:	Two-seater berlinetta

Frame:	Steel monoque with tubular steel rear sub-frame		Length:	167.3 in (4,250 mm)
Front suspension:	Independent, unequal-length wishbones, coil springs, telescopic shock absorbers, anti-roll bar		Width:	74.8 in (1,900 mm)
			Height:	46.1 in (1,170 mm)
Rear suspension:	Independent, unequal-length wishbones, coil springs, telescopic shock absorbers, anti-roll bar		Weight:	2,976 lb (1,350 kg)
			Fuel tank capacity:	23 gal (88 liters)
Steering:	Rack and pinion			
Front/rear brakes :	Ventilated discs			
Wheels:	18-in magnesium alloy rims with 225/40 (front) and 265/40 (rear) tires			

DIMENSIONS AND WEIGHT

Wheelbase:	96.5 in (2,450 mm)
Front/rear track:	59.6/63.6 in (1,514/1,615 mm)

PERFORMANCE

Top speed:	183 mph (295 km/h)
Acceleration 0 to 60 mph (0 to 100 km/h):	4.7 seconds
Weight/power ratio:	7.83 lb/hp (3.55 kg/hp)

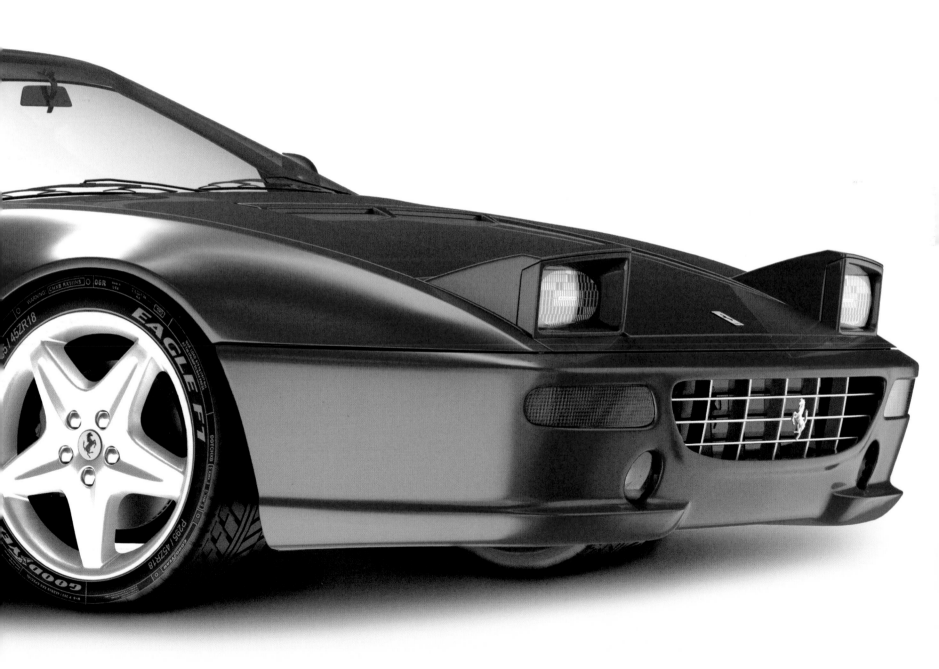

FERRARI F50

1995

Of all the Ferrari road cars, this was the one that came the closest to being a Formula One racer. Successor to the F40, this too was a celebration model, this time heralding fifty years of Ferrari as a car manufacturer. Technically, it was fundamentally very different from the F40. The engine was no longer a turbocharged V8, but a normally aspirated, tight 65° V12 with titanium alloy con-rods and five valves per cylinder derived from the power unit of the F1-90 Formula One car of 1990.

Displacement was increased from 213 to 287 cu in (3,498 to 4,698 cc). The chassis-frame was also very different. The F40 tubular steel frame with composite components gave way to a carbon fiber monocoque chassis, and the engine was used as a load-bearing member for the transmission and rear suspension. Designed by Pininfarina, the body was made entirely from composite materials and had a removable hardtop roof panel. The electronically controlled pushrod suspension was another crossover development from F1

and featured wishbones supporting the wheel-hub knuckles. A diagonal strut connected to the wheel-knuckle assembly was in turn connected to a rocker arm hinged to the coil spring and damper assembly. The spring-and-damper unit was horizontally mounted. Just like the F40, the only concession to comfort was air conditioning. The F50 did not have power steering, power-assisted braking, or ABS. An uncompromising, purist car, but less extreme than its predecessor.

The car went out of production in 1997.

TECHNICAL DATA

ENGINE

Type:	Central, longitudinal
Cylinders:	V12 (65°)
Bore x stroke:	3.35 x 2.72 in (85.0 x 69.0 mm)
Displacement:	287 cu in (4,698 cc)
Maximum power:	520 hp at 8,500 rpm
Maximum torque:	348 lb-ft (48.1 kgm) at 6,500 rpm
Valve actuation:	Twin overhead camshafts per bank
Valves:	Five per cylinder
Fuel feed:	Bosch Motronic M2.7 electronic fuel injection
Ignition:	Bosch Motronic M2.7 static electronic, single spark plug per cylinder
Cooling:	Water-cooled
Lubrication:	Dry sump

TRANSMISSION

Drive:	Rear-wheel drive
Clutch:	Twin-plate
Gearbox:	Manual, 6-speed + reverse

CHASSIS

Bodywork:	Two-seater spider
Frame:	Carbon fiber monocoque
Front suspension:	Independent pushrod, double wishbones, coil springs, telescopic shock absorbers
Rear suspension:	Independent pushrod, double wishbones, coil springs, telescopic shock absorbers
Steering:	Rack and pinion
Front/rear brakes:	Drilled, ventilated discs
Wheels:	18-in magnesium alloy rims with 245/35 (front) and 335/30 (rear) tires

DIMENSIONS AND WEIGHT

Wheelbase:	101.6 in (2,580 mm)
Front/rear track:	63.8/63.1 in (1,620/1,602 mm)
Length:	176.4 in (4,480 mm)
Width:	78.2 in (1,986 mm)
Height:	44.1 in (1,120 mm)
Weight:	2,712 lb (1,230 kg)
Fuel tank capacity:	28 gal (105 liters)

PERFORMANCE

Top speed:	202 mph (325 km/h)
Acceleration 0 to 60 mph (0 to 100 km/h):	3.87 seconds
Weight/power ratio:	5.20 lb/hp (2.36 kg/hp)

FERRARI 360 MODENA

1999

Successor to the F355, this new car was a radical departure from the past in terms of both technology and styling. It saw the introduction of a new styling approach at Ferrari, with a completely new aerodynamic line. The front inlet grilles channeled air to the radiators, allowing the airflow to pass under the raised center section, directing it to the rear suspension assembly via the undertray and then to extractors under its tail. This increased the car's downforce at high speed.

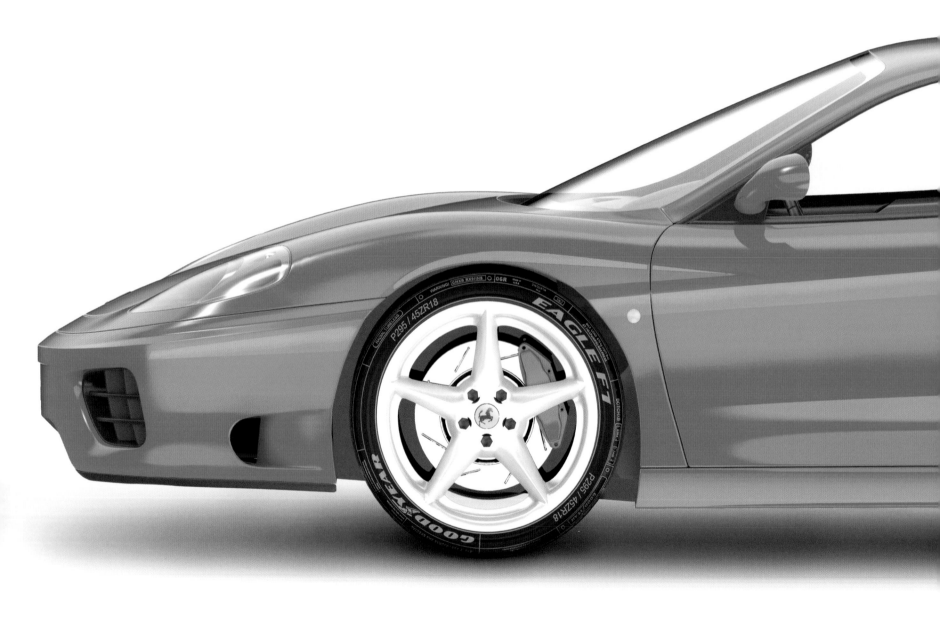

This was the first road-going Ferrari to feature a fully aluminum monocoque, 40% more rigid than the steel monocoque of the F355. Further reductions in weight were made by the use of aluminum for the body panels. The 360 Modena thus weighed in at 2,844 lb (1,290 kg), 132 lb (60 kg) lighter than its predecessor despite being dimensionally larger: it was 8.9 in (22.7 cm) longer than the F355. There was also an increase in wheelbase from 96.4 in to 102.4 in (2,450 to 2,600 mm). This model also saw the debut of electronic traction control which, like the electronic suspension control, had various settings. Electronic control could be switched off completely for competition. In comparison with the F355, the displacement of the 40-valve V8 power unit was increased to 220 cu in (3.6 liters), hence the "360" in the model name. Another innovation was the fly-by-wire throttle system, a fully electronic system without any mechanical connections. The car went out of production in 2004 and was replaced by the F430.

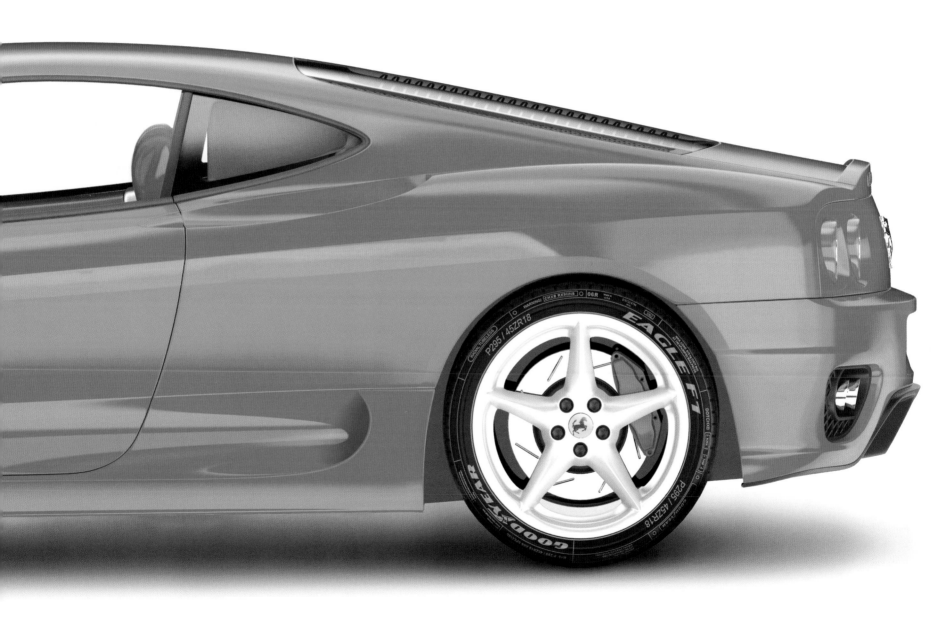

TECHNICAL DATA

ENGINE

Type:	Central, longitudinal
Cylinders:	V8 (90°)
Bore x stroke:	3.35 x 3.11 in (85.0 x 79.0 mm)
Displacement:	219 cu in (3,586 cc)
Maximum power:	400 hp at 8,500 rpm
Maximum torque:	276 lb-ft (38.1 kgm) at 4,750 rpm
Valve actuation:	Twin overhead camshafts per bank
Valves:	Five per cylinder

Fuel feed:	Bosch Motronic ME7.3 electronic fuel injection
Ignition:	Bosch Motronic ME7.3 static electronic, single spark plug per cylinder
Cooling:	Water-cooled
Lubrication:	Dry sump

TRANSMISSION

Drive:	Rear-wheel drive
Clutch:	Dry single-plate
Gearbox:	Manual, 6-speed + reverse (also with F1 electro-hydraulic 6-speed + reverse)

CHASSIS

Bodywork:	Two-seater berlinetta
Frame:	Aluminum space frame
Front suspension:	Independent, unequal-length wishbones, coil springs, telescopic shock absorbers, anti-roll bar
Rear suspension:	Independent, unequal-length wishbones, coil springs, telescopic shock absorbers, anti-roll bar
Steering:	Rack and pinion
Front/rear brakes:	Ventilated discs
Wheels:	18-in light alloy rims with 215/45 (front) and 275/40 (rear) tires

DIMENSIONS AND WEIGHT

Wheelbase:	102.4 in (2,600 mm)
Front/rear track:	65.7/63.7 in (1,669/1,617 mm)
Length:	176.3 in (4,477 mm)
Width:	75.7 in (1,922 mm)
Height:	47.8 in (1,214 mm)
Weight:	2,844 lb (1,290 kg)
Fuel tank capacity:	25 gal (95 liters)

PERFORMANCE

Top speed:	183 mph (295 km/h)
Acceleration 0 to 60 mph (0 to 100 km/h):	4.5 seconds
Weight/power ratio:	7.10 lb/hp (3.22 kg/hp)

FERRARI 360
SPIDER

2000

TECHNICAL DATA

ENGINE

Type:	Central, longitudinal
Cylinders:	V8 (90°)
Bore x stroke:	3.35 x 3.11 in (85.0 x 79.0 mm)
Displacement:	219 cu in (3,586 cc)
Maximum power:	400 hp at 8,500 rpm
Maximum torque:	276 lb-ft (38.1 kgm) at 4,750 rpm
Valve actuation:	Twin overhead camshafts per bank
Valves:	Five per cylinder
Fuel feed:	Bosch Motronic ME7.3 electronic fuel injection
Ignition:	Bosch Motronic ME7.3 static electronic, single spark plug per cylinder
Cooling:	Water-cooled
Lubrication:	Dry sump

TRANSMISSION

Drive:	Rear-wheel drive
Clutch:	Dry single-plate
Gearbox:	Manual, 6-speed + reverse (also with F1 electro-hydraulic 6-speed + reverse)

CHASSIS

Bodywork:	Two-seater spider
Frame:	Aluminum space frame
Front suspension:	Independent, unequal-length wishbones, coil springs, telescopic shock absorbers, anti-roll bar
Rear suspension:	Independent, unequal-length wishbones, coil springs, telescopic shock absorbers, anti-roll bar
Steering:	Rack and pinion
Front/rear brakes:	Ventilated discs
Wheels:	18-in light alloy rims with 215/45 (front) and 275/40 (rear) tires

DIMENSIONS AND WEIGHT

Wheelbase:	102.4 in (2,600 mm)
Front/rear track:	65.7/63.7 in (1,669/1,617 mm)
Length:	176.3 in (4,477 mm)
Width:	75.7 in (1,922 mm)
Height:	48.6 in (1,235 mm)
Weight:	2,976 lb (1,350 kg)
Fuel tank capacity:	25 gal (95 liters)

PERFORMANCE

Top speed:	Over 180 mph (290 km/h)
Acceleration 0 to 60 mph (0 to 100 km/h):	4.6 seconds
Weight/power ratio:	7.43 lb/hp (3.37 kg/hp)

Successor to the F355 Spider, this car had the same front design and aerodynamic styling as the 360 Modena coupé. Aerodynamic efficiency was obtained by channeling the airflow through the front inlet grilles to the radiators, and then under the raised center section via an undertray to channel air beneath the car to extractors under the tail. This solution derived from Ferrari's experience on the Formula One track increased downforce at high speed without the need to interfere with the clean, aerodynamic styling of this spider from Maranello. Opening and closing of the fabric top was fully automatic and, powered by an electric motor, took less than 20 seconds. The complete convertible top mechanism, like that on the F355 Spider, folds

away in a small space between the cabin and the mid-mounted V8. This time, however, there was a difference: the convertible-top components were no longer protected by a layer of fabric, but instead by two metal dorsal fins topped by rollbars. The aluminum monocoque was similar to that of the coupé but was stiffened at the front and rear. This increased the Spider's weight by 132 lb (60 kg). The suspension and mechanical components remained as before on the berlinetta. The outstanding feature of this vehicle is undoubtedly the V8, 5-valves-per-cylinder, 220 cu in (3.6 liter) engine delivering 400 hp and a torque of 276 lb-ft (38.1 kgm). The car went out of production in 2005, being replaced by the F430 Spider.

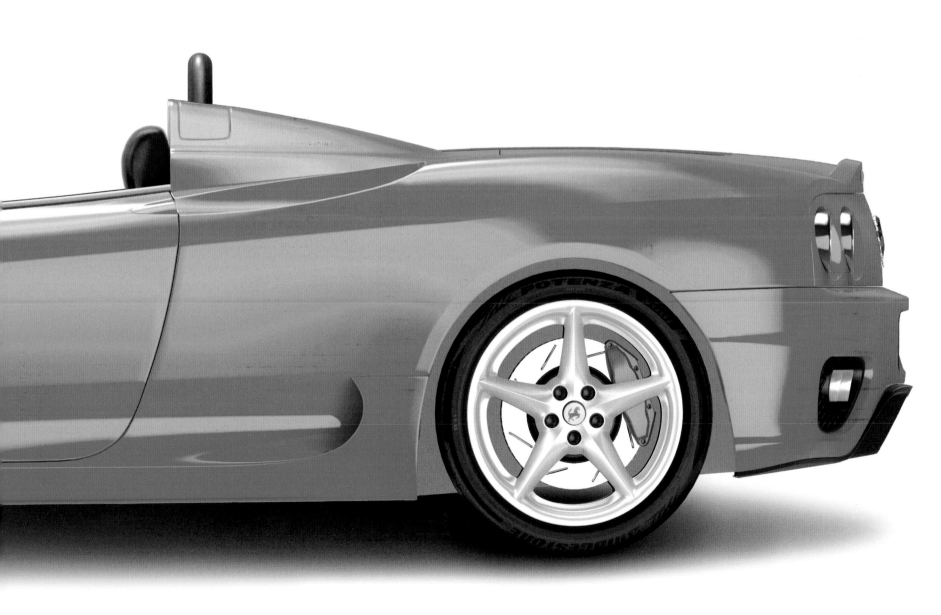

FERRARI 550 BARCHETTA PININFARINA

2000

A name that conjures up the past. "Barchetta" evokes the spider 166 MM of the nineteen-forties. "Pininfarina" was celebrating the upcoming 50th anniversary of the collaboration between Ferrari and the Turin-based coachbuilder and stylist. At the top of the wish list for Ferrari's president Luca Cordero di Montezemolo, this was a strictly limited edition of just 448 numbered units, an open-top version of the 550 Maranello berlinetta. The 550 Maranello, the ideal successor to the 365 GTB/4 Daytona, was powered by the classic front-mounted V12. This engine was the powerful 334 cu in (5,474 cc) unit delivering 485 hp, with the variable-geometry intake manifolds, cylinder block, cylinder heads, and sump all made of aluminum.

Light alloy was also used for the bodywork. The manual 6-speed gearbox was a transaxle type: that is, mounted as a unit with the differential to the rear axle.

Other features included electronic suspension control and multi-parameter traction control. A simple, manual soft-top for emergency use only made it possible to keep the car's weight down compared to that of the berlinetta, despite the additional strengthening of the chassis and hoop rollbars. This provided a weight-to-power ratio of 7.7 lb/hp (3.48 kg/hp). The windshield was 10 cm lower and had a steeper angle than that of the 550 Maranello. The tubular steel chassis frame was the same on both vehicles.

TECHNICAL DATA

ENGINE

Type:	Front, longitudinal
Cylinders:	V12 (65°)
Bore x stroke:	3.46 x 2.95 in (88.0 x 75.0 mm)
Displacement:	344 cu in (5,474 cc)
Maximum power:	485 hp at 7,000 rpm
Maximum torque:	420 lb-ft (58.1 kgm) at 5,000 rpm
Valve actuation:	Twin overhead camshafts per bank
Valves:	Four per cylinder
Fuel feed:	Bosch Motronic M5.2 electronic fuel injection
Ignition:	Bosch Motronic M5.2 static electronic, single spark plug per cylinder
Cooling:	Water-cooled
Lubrication:	Dry sump

TRANSMISSION

Drive:	Rear-wheel drive
Clutch:	Dry single-plate
Gearbox:	Manual, 6-speed + reverse

CHASSIS

Bodywork:	Two-seater barchetta
Frame:	Tubular steel
Front suspension:	Independent, double wishbones, coil springs, telescopic shock absorbers, anti-roll bar
Rear suspension:	Independent, double wishbones, coil springs, telescopic shock absorbers, anti-roll bar
Steering:	Rack and pinion
Front/rear brakes:	Ventilated discs
Wheels:	18-in light alloy rims with 255/40 (front) and 295/35 (rear) tires

DIMENSIONS AND WEIGHT

Wheelbase:	98.4 in (2,500 mm)
Front/rear track:	64.3/62.4 in (1,632/1,586 mm)
Length:	179.1 in (4,550 mm)
Width:	76.2 in (1,935 mm)
Height:	49.5 in (1,258 mm)
Weight:	3,726 lb (1,690 kg)
Fuel tank capacity:	30 gal (114 liters)

PERFORMANCE

Top speed:	186 mph (300 km/h)
Acceleration 0 to 60 mph (0 to 100 km/h):	4.4 seconds
Weight/power ratio:	7.67 lb/hp (3.48 kg/hp)

A V12 front-engine sports berlinetta—a Ferrari classic. The 575M Maranello represents the very pinnacle of technical excellence and performance. The name 575 referred to the displacement of the V12 (5.75 liters), and the letter M stood for "Modified," indicating that the car incorporated modifications to practically every aspect of its 550 Maranello predecessor. The displacement of the 550 power unit was increased from 334 to 351 cu in (5,474 cc to 5,748 cc). This modification, combined with optimization of the intake system and raising of the compression ratio from 10.8:1 to 11.0:1, boosted engine output from 485 hp to 515 hp and the torque from 420 to 434 lb-ft (from 58.1 to 60.0 kgm). This was also the first time that a road-going V12 Ferrari was available with a 6-speed F1-style electro-hydraulic gear change. Designed by Pininfarina, the 575M Maranello also boasted optimal weight distribution, with a 50-50 split between the axles with the driver onboard. This was aided by the transaxle design, which had the rear-mounted gearbox in unit with the limited-slip differential. The new car borrowed the new high-performance adaptive damping system first seen on the Ferrari Enzo, and featured independent electronic control on each wheel. Interiors were luxurious and sporty.

In 2006, it was replaced by the 599 GTB Fiorano.

FERRARI 575M MARANELLO

2002

TECHNICAL DATA

ENGINE

Type:	Front, longitudinal
Cylinders:	V12 (65°)
Bore x stroke:	3.50 x 3.03 in (89.0 x 77.0 mm)
Displacement:	351 cu in (5,748 cc)
Maximum power:	515 hp at 7,250 rpm
Maximum torque:	434 lb-ft (60.0 kgm) at 5,250 rpm
Valve actuation:	Twin overhead camshafts per bank
Valves:	Four per cylinder
Fuel feed:	Bosch Motronic M7.1 electronic fuel injection
Ignition:	Bosch Motronic M7.1 static electronic, single spark plug per cylinder
Cooling:	Water-cooled
Lubrication:	Dry sump

TRANSMISSION

Drive:	Rear-wheel drive
Clutch:	Dry single-plate
Gearbox:	Manual, 6-speed + reverse (also with F1 electro-hydraulic 6-speed + reverse)

CHASSIS

Bodywork:	Two-seater berlinetta
Frame:	Tubular steel
Front suspension:	Independent, double wishbones, coil springs, telescopic shock absorbers, anti-roll bar
Rear suspension:	Independent, double wishbones, coil springs, telescopic shock absorbers, anti-roll bar
Steering:	Rack and pinion
Front/rear brakes:	Ventilated discs
Wheels:	18-in light alloy rims with 255/40 (front) and 295/35 (rear) tires

DIMENSIONS AND WEIGHT

Wheelbase:	98.4 in (2,500 mm)
Front/rear track:	64.3/62.4 in (1,632/1,586 mm)
Length:	179.1 in (4,550 mm)
Width:	76.2 in (1,935 mm)
Height:	50.3 in (1,277 mm)
Weight:	3,814 lb (1,730 kg)
Fuel tank capacity:	28 gal (105 liters)

PERFORMANCE

Top speed:	202 mph (325 km/h)
Acceleration 0 to 60 mph (0 to 100 km/h):	4.2 seconds
Weight/power ratio:	7.41 lb/hp (3.36 kg/hp)

FERRARI ENZO

2002

The sportscar world would never be the same after the Enzo. Those who believed that the F40 and F50 had reached the pinnacle of performance in a road-legal supercar had to think again. The Ferrari Enzo not only commemorated Enzo Ferrari, who had died in 1988, but it also incorporated state-of-the-art Formula 1 technology in a road car. The front-end design and the carbon-fiber-and-aluminum-honeycomb-sandwich monocoque were clearly inspired by Ferrari's single-seater race cars. The mid-mounted 65° V12 engine had the same number of cylinders and architecture as a standard Ferrari V12, but the similarities ended there. The rest of the engine was derived directly from F1 racing engines. The displacement of 366 cu in (5,998 cc) produced some astonishing performance figures: 660 hp, 0–60 mph (0–100 km/h) in 3.65 seconds, a top speed of 217 mph (350 km/h), and a weight/power ratio of 4.2 lb/hp (1.90 kg/hp). The gearbox was the well-known 6-speed electro-hydraulic F1 unit developed to make a gear change in 150 milliseconds. This was the first Ferrari road car to be fitted with carbon-ceramic (CCM) discs produced by the specialist Italian brake maker, Brembo. Controls for the traction control and the SSC (side slip angle control) were built into the steering wheel. Designed by Pininfarina, the Enzo shared the electronically controlled pushrod suspension, with the difference being that this time the control was adaptive. The car weighed just 2,767 lb (1,255kg), thanks also to bodywork made from carbon fiber throughout. The aerodynamic ground effect was guaranteed by interaction between the flat undertray, the extractor, the flap, and the variable-angle spoiler. A total of 399 units were produced.

TECHNICAL DATA

ENGINE

Type:	Central, longitudinal
Cylinders:	V12 (65°)
Bore x stroke:	3.62 x 2.96 in (92.0 x 75.2 mm)
Displacement:	366 cu in (5,998 cc)
Maximum power:	660 hp at 7,800 rpm
Maximum torque:	485 lb-ft (67.0 kgm) at 5,500 rpm
Valve actuation:	Twin overhead camshafts per bank
Valves:	Four per cylinder
Fuel feed:	Bosch Motronic ME7 electronic fuel injection
Ignition:	Bosch Motronic ME7 static electronic, single spark plug per cylinder
Cooling:	Water-cooled
Lubrication:	Dry sump

TRANSMISSION

Drive:	Rear-wheel drive
Clutch:	Twin-plate
Gearbox:	F1 electro-hydraulic 6-speed + reverse

CHASSIS

Bodywork:	Two-seater berlinetta
Frame:	Carbon fiber and aluminum honeycomb monococque
Front suspension:	Independent pushrod, double wishbones, coil springs, telescopic shock absorbers
Rear suspension:	Independent pushrod, double wishbones, coil springs, telescopic shock absorbers
Steering:	Rack and pinion
Front/rear brakes:	Carbon-ceramic discs
Wheels:	19-in magnesium alloy rims with 245/35 (front) and 345/35 (rear) tires

DIMENSIONS AND WEIGHT

Wheelbase:	104.3 in (2,650 mm)
Front/rear track:	65.4/65.0 in (1,660/1,650 mm)
Length:	185.1 in (4,702 mm)
Width:	80.1 in (2,035 mm)
Height:	45.2 in (1,147 mm)
Weight:	2,767 lb (1,255 kg)
Fuel tank capacity:	29 gal (110 liters)

PERFORMANCE

Top speed:	Over 217 mph (350 km/h)
Acceleration 0 to 60 mph (0 to 100 km/h):	3.65 seconds
Weight/power ratio:	4.19 lb/hp (1.90 kg/hp)

FERRARI 612 SCAGLIETTI

2004

TECHNICAL DATA

ENGINE

Type:	Front, longitudinal
Cylinders:	V12 (65°)
Bore x stroke:	3.50 x 3.03 in (89.0 x 77.0 mm)
Displacement:	351 cu in (5,748 cc)
Maximum power:	540 hp at 7,250 rpm
Maximum torque:	434 lb-ft (60.0 kgm) at 5,250 rpm
Valve actuation:	Twin overhead camshafts per bank
Valves:	Four per cylinder
Fuel feed:	Bosch Motronic ME7 electronic fuel injection
Ignition:	Bosch Motronic ME7 static electronic, single spark plug per cylinder
Cooling:	Water-cooled
Lubrication:	Dry sump

TRANSMISSION

Drive:	Rear-wheel drive
Clutch:	Dry single-plate
Gearbox:	F1 electro-hydraulic 6-speed + reverse

CHASSIS

Bodywork:	2+2 coupé

Frame:	Aluminum monocoque
Front suspension:	Independent, double wishbones, coil springs, telescopic shock absorbers, anti-roll bar
Rear suspension:	Independent, double wishbones, coil springs, telescopic shock absorbers, anti-roll bar
Steering:	Rack and pinion
Front/rear brakes:	Ventilated discs
Wheels:	Front: 18-in alloy rims wheels with 245/45 tires Rear: 19-in alloy rims with 285/40 tires

DIMENSIONS AND WEIGHT

Wheelbase:	116.1 in (2,950 mm)
Front/rear track:	66.5/64.6 in (1,688/1,641 mm)
Length:	193.0 in (4,902 mm)
Width:	77.0 in (1,957 mm)
Height:	52.9 in (1,344 mm)
Weight:	4,123 lb (1,840 kg)
Fuel tank capacity:	28.5 gal (108 liters)

PERFORMANCE

Top speed:	199 mph (320 km/h)
Acceleration 0 to 60 mph (0 to 100 km/h):	4.2 seconds
Weight/power ratio:	7.52 lb/hp (3.41 kg/hp)

The successor to the 456 M with the same 2+2 configuration. Designed by Pininfarina, this car was named in memory of the late Sergio Scaglietti (1920–2011), the Modenese stylist and coachbuilder responsible for some of the most fascinating Ferraris of the nineteen-fifties and sixties.

As an homage to Scaglietti, a coachbuilder of consummate skill and a wizard with sheet aluminum, the car was made entirely of aluminum and featured lines resembling the 1954 375 MM, a car commissioned by the film director Roberto Rossellini for his wife, actress Ingrid Bergman. The model number 612 referred to the displacement (6 liters) and the number of cylinders (12). It was also an homage to a car of the same name, the 612 Can Am, a 1968 prototype built for the Can-Am Challenge Cup series in the United States.

The bodywork style was that of a berlinetta, but the cabin, which could comfortably seat four, was worthy of a limousine. The interior could be completely personalized with custom features, including different types of dash inserts and natural, full-grain leather upholstery. The car was powered by the same front-mounted 351 cu in (5,748 cc) V12 as the 575 M Maranello, increased from 515 hp to 540 hp and fitted with an F1-style electro-hydraulic gearbox. The trans-axle transmission had the rear-mounted gearbox in unit with the limited-slip differential. Altogether nothing new for a Ferrari, except for the revolutionary electrochromic panoramic roof with three tint-level settings. A true innovation.

FERRARI P4/5
BY PININFARINA

2006

Unique in the true sense, this was a one-off sports car designed by the Turin coachbuilder Pininfarina for the American car collector James Glickenhaus. Technically, this was a Ferrari Enzo; but over 200 components were specially designed for this car to give it the appearance of the legendary 330 P3/4 prototype, the undisputed victor of the 24 Hours of Daytona in 1967. Officially presented to the public at the Pebble Beach Concours d'Elégance in 2006, the central

part of the body was dominated by a single-piece shell that included the windshield. Access to the cabin was through butterfly doors. Another striking feature was the transparent, drop-shaped rear window, which also acted as the engine cover. The exhaust pipes had a white ceramic coating just like the competition cars of the sixties. The bodywork was made entirely of carbon fiber, just like that of the car from which it was derived. Like the Enzo, it had the mid-mounted 65° V12 borrowed directly from F1 with a displacement of 366 cu in (5,998 cc)

and a power output of 660 hp. The wheels were 20-in rather than the 19-in rims of the Enzo, and the weight was reduced from the original 2,767 lb down to 2,646 lb (1,255 kg to 1,200 kg).

This resulted in a changed weight/power ratio from 4.18 lb/hp to 4.01 lb/hp (1.90 kg/hp to 1.82 kg/hp). Acceleration from 0 to 60 mph (0 to 100 km/h) was 3.55 seconds compared with 3.65 seconds. Maximum speed topped out at 225 mph (362 km/h). The price, never made official, was more than €3 million.

TECHNICAL DATA

ENGINE

Type:	Central, longitudinal
Cylinders:	V12 (65°)
Bore x stroke:	3.62 x 2.96 in (92.0 x 75.2 mm)
Displacement:	366 cu in (5,998 cc)
Maximum power:	660 hp at 7,800 rpm
Maximum torque:	485 lb-ft (67.0 kgm) at 5,500 rpm
Valve actuation:	Twin overhead camshafts per bank
Valves:	Four per cylinder
Fuel feed:	Bosch Motronic ME7 electronic fuel injection

Ignition:	Bosch Motronic ME7 static electronic, single spark plug per cylinder
Cooling:	Water-cooled
Lubrication:	Dry sump

TRANSMISSION

Drive:	Rear-wheel drive
Clutch:	Twin-plate
Gearbox:	F1 electro-hydraulic 6-speed + reverse

CHASSIS

Bodywork:	Two-seater berlinetta

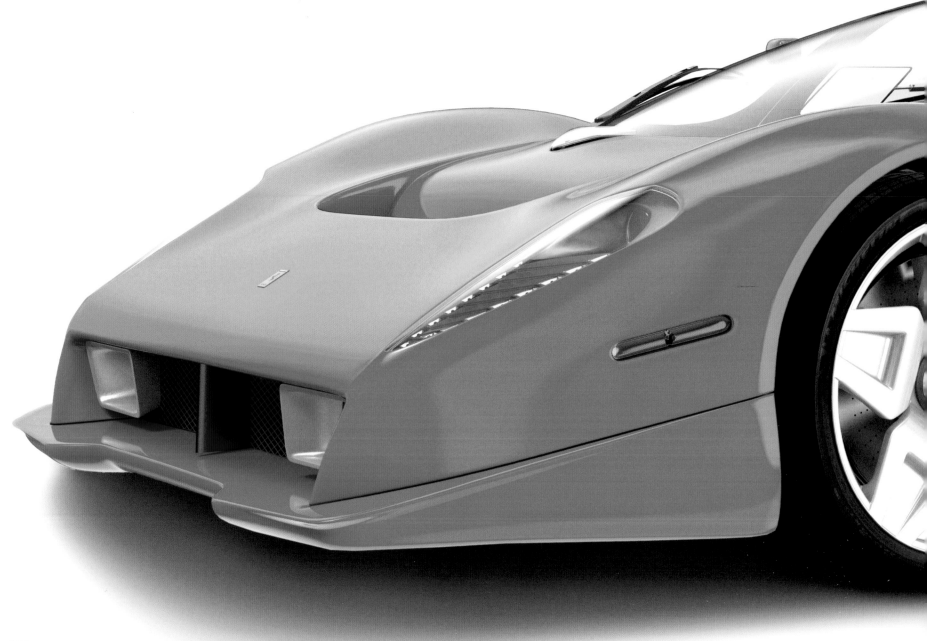

Frame:	Carbon fiber and aluminum honeycomb monococque
Front suspension:	Independent pushrod, double wishbones, coil springs, telescopic shock absorbers
Rear suspension:	Independent pushrod, double wishbones, coil springs, telescopic shock absorbers
Steering:	Rack and pinion
Front/rear brakes:	Carbon-ceramic discs
Wheels:	20-in light alloy rims with 255/35 (front) and 335/30 (rear) tires

DIMENSIONS AND WEIGHT

Wheelbase:	104.3 in (2,650 mm)

Front/rear track:	66.5/67.2 in (1,691/1,707 mm)
Length:	182.3 in (4,630 mm)
Width:	80.4 in (2,042 mm)
Height:	44.3 in (1,126 mm)
Weight:	2,646 lb (1,200 kg)
Fuel tank capacity:	29 gal (110 liters)

PERFORMANCE

Top speed:	225 mph (362 km/h)
Acceleration 0 to 60 mph (0 to 100 km/h):	3.55 seconds
Weight/power ratio:	4.01 lb/hp (1.82 kg/hp)

FERRARI 599 GTB FIORANO

2007

This car takes its name from the Ferrari test circuit at Fiorano near the Maranello production facility. "GTB" is a tribute to the legendary Gran Turismo Berlinetta, and "599" stands for the displacement (5,999 cc) of the V12 engine. Designed by Pininfarina, this was the heir to the 575M Maranello and saw the return of a Ferrari classic: the V12 front-engine sports berlinetta. The power unit was derived from the Enzo, with the output raised from 620 to 660 hp. The gearbox was the 6-speed, electro-hydraulic F1 unit developed to make gear changes in 100 milliseconds, a considerable improvement over the 250 milliseconds of the 575M Maranello. A major technical innovation on this car was the introduction of magnetorheological suspension, a system where the shock absorbers control the damping action on the compression and extension strokes by instantly varying the viscosity of the fluid inside the shock absorbers. An electronically controlled magnetic field varies the viscosity of the fluid and therefore the damping action to match the driving style and program selected. The system was a true revolution in terms of suspension response times, particularly in comparison with traditional damper systems regulated by compensation valves. The 599 GTB was to be used as the platform for future variants and high-performance developments, including the HGTE, GTO, SA Aperta, XX Evoluzione, and also the 599 GTB HY-KERS hybrid concept car.

TECHNICAL DATA

ENGINE

Type:	Front, longitudinal
Cylinders:	V12 (65°)
Bore x stroke:	3.62 x 2.96 in (92.0 x 75.2 mm)
Displacement:	366 cu in (5,999 cc)
Maximum power:	620 hp at 7,600 rpm
Maximum torque:	448 lb-ft (62.0 kgm) at 5,600 rpm
Valve actuation:	Twin overhead camshafts per bank
Valves:	Four per cylinder

Fuel feed:	Bosch Motronic ME7 electronic fuel injection
Ignition:	Bosch Motronic ME7 static electronic, single spark plug per cylinder
Cooling:	Water-cooled
Lubrication:	Dry sump

TRANSMISSION

Drive:	Rear-wheel drive
Clutch:	Twin-plate
Gearbox:	F1 electro-hydraulic, 6-speed + reverse/Manual, 6-speed + reverse

CHASSIS

Bodywork:	Two-seater berlinetta
Frame:	Aluminum space frame
Front suspension:	Independent, double wishbones, coil springs, telescopic shock absorbers, anti-roll bar
Rear suspension:	Independent, double wishbones, coil springs, telescopic shock absorbers, anti-roll bar
Steering:	Rack and pinion
Front/rear brakes:	Carbon-ceramic discs
Wheels:	Front: 19-in alloy rims wheels with 245/40 tires
	Rear: 20-in alloy rims with 305/35 tires

DIMENSIONS AND WEIGHT

Wheelbase:	108.3 in (2,750 mm)
Front/rear track:	66.5/63.7 in (1,690/1,618 mm)
Length:	183.7 in (4,665 mm)
Width:	77.2 in (1,962 mm)
Height:	52.6 in (1,336 mm)
Weight:	3,483 lb (1,580 kg)
Fuel tank capacity:	28 gal (105 liters)

PERFORMANCE

Top speed:	over 205 mph (330 km/h)
Acceleration 0 to 60 mph (0 to 100 km/h):	3.7 seconds
Weight/power ratio:	5.62 lb/hp (2.55 kg/hp)

In 2004, the F430 took the place of the 360 Modena and saw the debut of technological innovations including the electronic differential and the manettino dial control. The celebrated dial control on the steering wheel is used to manage the programming of the stability and traction control, the limited-slip differential, the gearbox, the ABS, and the suspension settings. After three years of honorable service, the F430 was joined by a racing-oriented Scuderia version, similar to what was done when the 360 Modena was joined by the Challenge Stradale.

Powered by the same 32-valve, 263 cu in (4,308 cc) V8, the original 490 hp and 343 lb-ft (47.4 kgm) of torque were raised to 510 hp and 346 lb-ft (47.9 kgm). The Scuderia was 220 lb (100 kg) lighter than the F430 and would accelerate from 0 to 60 mph (0 to 100 km/h) in 3.6 seconds. Top speed hit 199 mph (320 km/h). Developed with the assistance of F1 driver Michael Schumacher, the car was 0.6 in lower (15 mm) than the 430 and had more-rigid springs and shock absorbers.

The Scuderia had carbon-ceramic brake discs and the F1-Super-fast2 gearbox, the latest version of the F1 electro-hydraulic unit,

which now cut gear-change times from 150 to 60 milliseconds. The aerodynamics were further tuned with changes to the front air intakes, the sills, the integrated spoiler, the flat undertray, and the extractor. The objective here was to enhance down-force which, in the case of the Scuderia, now reached 661 lb (300 kg) at 199 mph (320 km/h). The interior design was simple and functional. Differences with respect to the F430 included carbon fiber door panels and a central tunnel. Alcantara replaced leather as upholstery. The Scuderia also saw the debut of composite fiber shell seats.

FERRARI 430 SCUDERIA

2007

TECHNICAL DATA

ENGINE

Type:	Central, longitudinal
Cylinders:	V8 (90°)
Bore x stroke:	3.62 x 3.19 in (92.0 x 81.0 mm)
Displacement:	263 cu in (4,308 cc)
Maximum power:	510 hp at 8,500 rpm
Maximum torque:	346 lb-ft (47.9 kgm) at 5,250 rpm
Valve actuation:	Twin overhead camshafts per bank
Valves:	Four per cylinder
Fuel feed:	Bosch Motronic ME7 electronic fuel injection
Ignition:	Bosch Motronic ME7 static electronic, single spark plug per cylinder
Cooling:	Water-cooled
Lubrication:	Dry sump

TRANSMISSION

Drive:	Rear-wheel drive
Clutch:	Twin-plate
Gearbox:	F1 electro-hydraulic 6-speed + reverse

CHASSIS

Bodywork:	Two-seater berlinetta
Frame:	Aluminum space frame
Front suspension:	Independent, double wishbones, coil springs, telescopic shock absorbers, anti-roll bar
Rear suspension:	Independent, double wishbones, coil springs, telescopic shock absorbers, anti-roll bar
Steering:	Rack and pinion
Front/rear brakes:	Carbon-ceramic discs
Wheels:	19-in light alloy rims with 235/35 (front) and 285/35 (rear) tires

DIMENSIONS AND WEIGHT

Wheelbase:	102.4 in (2,600 mm)
Front/rear track:	65.7/63.6 in (1,669/1,616 mm)
Length:	177.6 in (4,512 mm)
Width:	75.7 in (1,923 mm)
Height:	47.2 in (1,199 mm)
Weight:	2,756 lb (1,250 kg)
Fuel tank capacity:	25 gal (95 liters)

PERFORMANCE

Top speed:	199 mph (320 km/h)
Acceleration 0 to 60 mph (0 to 100 km/h):	3.6 seconds
Weight/power ratio:	5.40 lb/hp (2.45 kg/hp)

FERRARI CALIFORNIA

2008

TECHNICAL DATA

ENGINE

Type:	Front, longitudinal
Cylinders:	V8 (90°)
Bore x stroke:	3.90 x 3.05 in (99.0 x 77.4 mm)
Displacement:	262 cu in (4,297 cc)
Maximum power:	460 hp at 7,750 rpm
Maximum torque:	357 lb-ft (49.4 kgm) at 5,000 rpm
Valve actuation:	Twin overhead camshafts per bank
Valves:	Four per cylinder
Fuel feed:	Direct electronic fuel injection
Ignition:	Static electronic, one spark plug per cylinder
Cooling:	Water-cooled
Lubrication:	Dry sump

TRANSMISSION

Drive:	Rear-wheel drive
Clutch:	Dual
Gearbox:	Dual clutch (DCT), 7-speed + reverse

CHASSIS

Bodywork:	Two-seater coupé/cabriolet – 2+2
Frame:	Aluminum space frame
Front suspension:	Independent, double wishbones, coil springs, telescopic shock absorbers, anti-roll bar
Rear suspension:	Independent, multilink, coil springs, telescopic shock absorbers, anti-roll bar
Steering:	Rack and pinion
Front/rear brakes:	Carbon-ceramic discs
Wheels:	19-in light alloy rims with 245/40 (front) and 285/40 (rear) tires

DIMENSIONS AND WEIGHT

Wheelbase:	105.1 in (2,670 mm)
Front/rear track:	64.2/63.2 in (1,630/1,605 mm)
Length:	179.6 in (4,563 mm)
Width:	74.9 in (1,902 mm)
Height:	51.5 in (1,308 mm)
Weight:	3,825 lb/1,735 kg (curb weight)
Fuel tank capacity:	21 gal (78 liters)

PERFORMANCE

Top speed:	193 mph (310 km/h)
Acceleration 0 to 60 mph (0 to 100 km/h):	3.9 seconds
Weight/power ratio:	8.31 lb/hp (3.77 kg/hp)

The first Ferrari coupé-cabriolet, a roadster with a retractable hard top. The first front-engined Ferrari with a V8 in the position previously reserved for the classic Ferrari V12. The first Ferrari to be fitted with a dual-clutch transmission in place of the classic F1 electro-hydraulic unit. The first Ferrari with direct fuel injection. In short, this was the car that marked a break with the past, especially in technical terms, and one that introduced features that were to become "must-haves" on later vehicles from Maranello. Designed by Pininfarina, it took less than 14 seconds to pass from the coupé to the open-top configuration, thanks to the electrically controlled aluminum hard top, which disappeared from view into a compartment at the back of the cabin. It shared various features with other Ferrari production cars, including the manettino dial control previously introduced on the F430. This time, there were three driving programs rather than the five on the F430 and 599 GTB, giving the impression that this was intended as a grand touring sports car rather than something more extreme. The impression was confirmed by its weight: 3,825 lb (1,735 kg). The F1 electro-hydraulic gearbox was replaced by a 7-speed, dual-clutch transaxle transmission at the rear, which was produced by the German maker Getrag. A new feature was the rear suspension with a multilink system in place of the standard double wishbones. Magnetorheological shock absorbers, used for the first time on the 599 GTB Fiorano, were also available as an option. The original aspirated V8 has been replaced in 2014 by an even more powerful 8-cylinder with twin turbochargers. The new model took the name of California T and was produced from 2014 to 2018.

FERRARI 458 ITALIA

2009

TECHNICAL DATA

ENGINE

Type:	Central, longitudinal
Cylinders:	V8 (90°)
Bore x stroke:	3.70 x 3.19 in (94.0 x 81.0 mm)
Displacement:	275 cu in (4,499 cc)
Maximum power:	570 hp at 9,000 rpm
Maximum torque:	398 lb-ft (55.0 kgm) at 6,000 rpm
Valve actuation:	Twin overhead camshafts per bank
Valves:	Four per cylinder
Fuel feed:	Direct electronic fuel injection
Ignition:	Static electronic, one spark plug per cylinder
Cooling:	Water-cooled
Lubrication:	Dry sump

TRANSMISSION

Drive:	Rear-wheel drive
Clutch:	Dual
Gearbox:	Dual clutch (DCT), 7-speed + reverse

CHASSIS

Bodywork:	Two-seater berlinetta
Frame:	Aluminum space frame
Front suspension:	Independent, double wishbones, coil springs, telescopic shock absorbers, anti-roll bar

Rear suspension:	Independent, multilink, coil springs, telescopic shock absorbers, anti-roll bar
Steering:	Rack and pinion
Front/rear brakes:	Carbon-ceramic discs
Wheels:	20-in light alloy rims with 235/35 (front) and 295/35 (rear) tires

DIMENSIONS AND WEIGHT

Wheelbase:	104.3 in (2,650 mm)
Front/rear track:	65.8/63.2 in (1,672/1,606 mm)
Length:	178.2 in (4,527 mm)
Width:	76.3 in (1,937 mm)
Height:	47.8 in (1,213 mm)
Weight:	3,042 lb (1,380 kg)
Fuel tank capacity:	23 gal (86 liters)

PERFORMANCE

Top speed:	202 mph (325 km/h)
Acceleration 0 to 60 mph (0 to 100 km/h):	3.4 seconds
Weight/power ratio:	5.34 lb/hp (2.42 kg/hp)

Improve the F430. A seemingly impossible task, but one successfully completed in full by the 458 Italia. The 458 Italia is a berlinetta whose name indicates its displacement (4.5 liters or 275 cu in) and the number of cylinders (8) of the direct-injection engine. The V8 has a flat crankshaft, dry-sump lubrication, and racing solutions such as the graphite-coated piston skirts and the variable-geometry intake manifolds. These are fine-tuning developments which, combined with continuously variable timing on both the inlet and exhaust cams, enable the V8 to deliver 570 hp and 398 lb-ft (55.0 kgm) of torque. Designed by Pininfarina, the car's style marks a break with the past and a new beginning. This is clearly visible in the vertical stack of headlights, the integrated rear wing, and the central triple exhaust tailpipes at the rear. The cabin has been radically redesigned. The steering wheel hosts a whole range of controls, which has made it possible to adopt larger paddles controlling the 7-speed DCT dual-clutch gearbox (mounted in unit with the electronic differential). The 458 Italia also saw the debut of active aerodynamics in the form of the two small aeroelastic winglets on the nose. These deform at high speeds, changing angle to channel air to the radiators and increase downforce to 794 lb at 202 mph (360 kg at 325 km/h). The 458 Italia features the magnetorheological suspension system first introduced on the 599 GTB Fiorano. This controls damping by instantaneously varying the properties of a fluid inside the shock absorbers, which is sensitive to the magnetic field generated.

FERRARI P540 SUPERFAST APERTA

2009

The Golden Ferrari. This was the name given to a one-off based on a 599 GTB Fiorano and made by the Progetti Speciali-Special Projects department at Maranello.

The car with gold-colored paintwork was commissioned by Edward Walson, son of the inventor of cable TV, John Walson, who was inspired by the segment "Toby Dammit" directed by Federico Fellini in the 1968 omnibus film "Three Tales of the Macabre." In the film, actor Terence Stamp drives a gold-colored 1963 330 LMB, rebodied

by Fantuzzi. The P540 SuperFast Aperta, designed by Pininfarina, followed the basic idea of its predecessor but abandoned the berlinetta bodywork of the original in favor of a roadster configuration, as the model name "Aperta" (convertible) suggests.

This variation required stiffening the original 599 GTB chassis-frame in order to maintain torsional strength. Stiffening increased the weight of the Aperta, but only by 44 lb (20 kg). This was made possible by the massive use of carbon fiber. In addition to the paint-work color of the film's 330 LMB, the SuperFast Aperta shared the air vents behind the wheel arches, the flat roll-bar, the curvature of the hood, and the cut-off tail. Mechanically, the car was exactly the same as the 599 GTB.

This meant that it kept the same 366 cu in (6-liter) 620 hp V12 engine, the F1 6-speed electro-hydraulic gearbox, the magnetorheological shock absorbers, and the double-wishbone suspension front and rear.

TECHNICAL DATA

ENGINE

Type:	Front, longitudinal
Cylinders:	V12 (65°)
Bore x stroke:	3.62 x 2.96 in (92.0 x 75.2 mm)
Displacement:	366 cu in (5,999 cc)
Maximum power:	620 hp at 7,600 rpm
Maximum torque:	448 lb-ft (62.0 kgm) at 5,600 rpm
Valve actuation:	Twin overhead camshafts per bank

Valves:	Four per cylinder
Fuel feed:	Bosch Motronic ME7 electronic fuel injection
Ignition:	Bosch Motronic ME7 static electronic, single spark plug per cylinder
Cooling:	Water-cooled
Lubrication:	Dry sump

TRANSMISSION

Drive:	Rear-wheel drive
Clutch:	Twin-plate
Gearbox:	F1 electro-hydraulic 6-speed + reverse

CHASSIS

Bodywork:	Two-seater spider
Frame:	Aluminum space frame
Front suspension:	Independent, double wishbones, coil springs, telescopic shock absorbers, anti-roll bar
Rear suspension:	Independent, double wishbones, coil springs, telescopic shock absorbers, anti-roll bar
Steering:	Rack and pinion
Front/rear brakes:	Carbon-ceramic discs
Wheels:	20-in light alloy rims with 245/35 (front) and 305/35 (rear) tires

DIMENSIONS AND WEIGHT

Wheelbase:	108.3 in (2,750 mm)
Front/rear track:	66.5/63.8 in (1,690/1,620 mm)
Length:	186.3 in (4,731 mm)
Width:	76.9 in (1,954 mm)
Height:	51.2 in (1,300 mm)
Weight:	3,527 lb (1,600 kg)
Fuel tank capacity:	28 gal (105 liters)

PERFORMANCE

Top speed:	—
Acceleration 0 to 60 mph (0 to 100 km/h):	—
Weight/power ratio:	5.69 lb/hp (2.58 kg/hp)

FERRARI FF

2011

Four true seats and four-wheel drive. Close to a revolution. This was the real descendant of the 612 Scaglietti, saying goodbye to the 2+2 configuration to make way for a true four-seater which could comfortably accommodate four adults without any sacrifices. The FF was also the first Ferrari to use all-wheel drive. This was a solution that would keep purists happy, too. A gear system and a pair of continuous-slip, oil-bath multi-plate clutches take the torque directly from the engine

and only transmit it to the front wheels when required. This arrangement keeps the axles independent and therefore allows the vehicle to use rear-wheel drive under normal driving conditions. The multiplate clutches not only distribute the torque between the front and rear axles, but they also distribute power between the front wheels, simulating the action of a mechanical limited-slip differential.

Another innovation is the 382 cu in (6,262 cc) V12 with direct fuel injection and featuring a particularly high compression ratio (12.3:1) and a rated power output of 660 hp. The engine drives the well-known 7-speed, dual-clutch gearbox. The FF in the name stands for "Ferrari Four." Fitted with the latest version of the magnetorheological suspension and third generation carbon-ceramic brakes, the car also marked a strategic styling departure for Ferrari: this was the first Ferrari hatchback.

TECHNICAL DATA

ENGINE

Type:	Front, longitudinal
Cylinders:	V12 (65°)
Bore x stroke:	3.70 x 2.96 in (94.0 x 75.2 mm)
Displacement:	382 cu in (6,262 cc)
Maximum power:	660 hp at 8,000 rpm
Maximum torque:	504 lb-ft (69.7 kgm) at 6,000 rpm
Valve actuation:	Twin overhead camshafts per bank
Valves:	Four per cylinder
Fuel feed:	Direct electronic fuel injection

Ignition:	Static electronic, one spark plug per cylinder
Cooling:	Water-cooled
Lubrication:	Dry sump

TRANSMISSION

Drive:	Permanent four-wheel drive
Clutch:	Dual
Gearbox:	Dual clutch (DCT), 7-speed + reverse

CHASSIS

Bodywork:	Four-seater coupé
Frame:	Aluminum space frame

Front suspension:	Independent, double wishbones, coil springs, telescopic shock absorbers, anti-roll bar
Rear suspension:	Independent, multilink, coil springs, telescopic shock absorbers, anti-roll bar
Steering:	Rack and pinion
Front/rear brakes:	Carbon-ceramic discs
Wheels:	20-in light alloy rims with 245/35 (front) and 295/35 (rear) tires

DIMENSIONS AND WEIGHT

Wheelbase:	117.7 in (2,990 mm)

Front/rear track:	66.0/65.4 in (1,676/1,660 mm)
Length:	193.2 in (4,907 mm)
Width:	76.9 in (1,953 mm)
Height:	54.3 in (1,379 mm)
Weight:	3,946 lb (1,790 kg)
Fuel tank capacity:	24 gal (91 liters)

PERFORMANCE

Top speed:	208 mph (335 km/h)
Acceleration 0 to 60 mph (0 to 100 km/h):	3.7 seconds
Weight/power ratio:	5.97 lb/hp (2.71 kg/hp)

FERRARI SP12 EC

2012

An all-consuming passion for the 1976 512 BB berlinetta drove the British blues guitarist, singer, and songwriter Eric Clapton to commission a special version of the 458 Italia. This one-off, designed by the Ferrari Style Center at Maranello in collaboration with Pininfarina, has a characteristic opaque black lower body and has been completely restyled at the front and rear to evoke the 512 BB by which it is inspired.

Styling similarities with the 1976 model include a chromed grille at the front and triangular rear quarter lights. There are no similarities under the hood. The SP12 EC is powered by the same mid-mounted 275 cu in (4.5 liter) V8 as the 458 Italia, while the 512 BB berlinetta boxer boasted a 302 cu in (4,943 cc) V12. The English musician wanted to eliminate this discrepancy and asked for a V12 to be transplanted into the aluminum frame-chassis of the 2009 berlinetta. Ferrari technical designers had to disappoint him, citing the lack of space for the larger engine. As a partial consolation, the car was fitted with a personalized number plate with the model name and the initials EPC for Eric Patrick Clapton. The price of this one-off from Maranello? Rumors have it that the car cost over €3 million. The car's technical data are also strictly confidential.

TECHNICAL DATA

ENGINE

Type:	Central, longitudinal
Cylinders:	V8 (90°)
Bore x stroke:	3.70 x 3.19 in (94.0 x 81.0 mm)
Displacement:	275 cu in (4,499 cc)
Maximum power:	—
Maximum torque:	—
Valve actuation:	Twin overhead camshafts per bank
Valves:	Four per cylinder
Fuel feed:	Direct electronic fuel injection
Ignition:	Static electronic, one spark plug per cylinder
Cooling:	Water-cooled
Lubrication:	Dry sump

TRANSMISSION

Drive:	Rear-wheel drive
Clutch:	Dual
Gearbox:	Dual-clutch (DCT), 7-speed + reverse

CHASSIS

Bodywork:	Two-seater berlinetta
Frame:	Aluminum space frame
Front suspension:	Independent, double wishbones, coil springs, telescopic shock absorbers, anti-roll bar
Rear suspension:	Independent, multilink, coil springs, telescopic shock absorbers, anti-roll bar
Steering:	Rack and pinion
Front/rear brakes:	Carbon-ceramic discs
Wheels:	20-in light alloy rims with 235/35 (front) and 295/35 (rear) tires

DIMENSIONS AND WEIGHT

Wheelbase:	104.3 in (2,650 mm)
Front/rear track:	—
Length:	—
Width:	—
Height:	—
Weight:	—
Fuel tank capacity:	23 gal (86 liters)

PERFORMANCE

Top speed:	—
Acceleration 0 to 60 mph (0 to 100 km/h):	3.4 seconds
Weight/power ratio:	—

FERRARI 599XX EVOLUZIONE

2012

An extreme vehicle not approved for road use and designed exclusively for the racetrack. The XX Evoluzione is the successor to the 599XX of 2009 and, like its predecessor, is designed as a rolling laboratory for testing and developing new solutions that will later be transferred to series road cars. The car was reserved for customers-pilots who had the chance of driving the car to the limits in a private track-based program, backed by a dedicated official team. The car benefited from an

active aerodynamic package that included an electronically controlled rear wing where the angle of the wing flaps would adjust to match the track conditions. There were also a carbon-fiber extractor derived from Formula 1, and a large splitter made from composite material. At 200 km/h, these aerodynamic components created a downforce of 728 lb (330 kg) with the flaps open and 970 lb (440 kg) with the flaps closed. The 366 cu in (5,999 cc) V12 was not "choked" by catalyzers and

silencers, but had racing-type side exhausts. It delivered 750 hp and a torque of 516 lb-ft (71.4 kgm) in comparison with the 620 hp and 448 lb-ft (62.0 kgm) of its predecessor. Engine speed could reach a stratospheric 9,000 rpm. An astonishing weight/power ratio of 3.85 lb/hp (1.75 kg/hp) was made possible by slimming down the already ultralight 599XX by 77 lb (35 kg). The magnetorheological suspension was considerably stiffer than before. Slick tires were fitted.

TECHNICAL DATA

ENGINE

Type:	Front, longitudinal
Cylinders:	V12 (65°)
Bore x stroke:	3.62 x 2.96 in (92.0 x 75.2 mm)
Displacement:	366 cu in (5,999 cc)
Maximum power:	750 hp at 9,000 rpm
Maximum torque:	71.4 kg/hp
Valve actuation:	Twin overhead camshafts per bank
Valves:	Four per cylinder
Fuel feed:	Bosch Motronic ME7 electronic fuel injection
Ignition:	Bosch Motronic ME7 static electronic, single spark plug per cylinder
Cooling:	Water-cooled
Lubrication:	Dry sump

TRANSMISSION

Drive:	Rear-wheel drive
Clutch:	Twin-plate
Gearbox:	F1 electro-hydraulic 6-speed + reverse

CHASSIS

Bodywork:	Two-seater berlinetta
Frame:	Aluminum space frame
Front suspension:	Independent, double wishbones, coil springs, telescopic shock absorbers, anti-roll bar
Rear suspension:	Independent, double wishbones, coil springs, telescopic shock absorbers, anti-roll bar

Steering:	Rack and pinion		Height:	50.5 in (1,283 mm)
Front/rear brakes:	Carbon-ceramic discs		Weight:	2888 lb (1,310 kg)
Wheels:	19-in magnesium alloy rims with 29/67 (front) and 31/71 (rear) slick tires		Fuel tank capacity:	—

DIMENSIONS AND WEIGHT

Wheelbase:	108.3 in (2,750 mm)
Front/rear track:	—
Length:	188.5 in (4,787 mm)
Width:	77.6 in (1,972 mm)

PERFORMANCE

Top speed:	Over 208 mph (335 km/h)
Acceleration 0 to 60 mph (0 to 100 km/h):	—
Weight/power ratio:	3.85 lb/hp (1.75 kg/hp)

This is the most powerful Ferrari series road car of all time. This is the best front-engined V12 sports berlinetta ever to bear the Prancing Horse badge and yet another classic from Ferrari. Powered by the same 6,262 cc V12 as the FF, it boasts direct fuel injection and an astonishing compression ratio of 13.5:1. The completely new electronic control unit has a multi-spark ignition function which implements three successive sparks of different intensity and duration to optimize combustion. The engine puts out 740 hp and 509 lb-ft (70.4 kgm) of torque. More fluid, more compact, and 121 lb (55 kg) lighter than the 599 GTB Fiorano, which it replaces, the F12 has a much lower center of gravity thanks to an engine mounting which is 1.2 in lower (30 mm) than before. The F12 is the result of collaboration between the Centro Stile Ferrari-Style Center and Pininfarina. It has the same magnetorheological suspension as the FF and also shares the third-generation carbon-ceramic brakes now enhanced with an innovative dynamic cooling system at the front. The 7-speed, dual-clutch gearbox and the E-Diff electronic differential assure outstanding performance. Acceleration from 0 to 60 mph (0 to 100 km/h) takes just 3.1 seconds, 0 to 125 mph (0 to 200 km/h) takes 8.5 seconds, and maximum speed tops 211 mph (340 km/h). For the first time, hood design has made a contribution to creating downforce, which has been boosted by 76% in comparison with the 599 GTB.

FERRARI F12 BERLINETTA

2012

TECHNICAL DATA

ENGINE

Type:	Front, longitudinal
Cylinders:	V12 (65°)
Bore x stroke:	3.70 x 2.96 in (94.0 x 75.2 mm)
Displacement:	382 cu in (6,262 cc)
Maximum power:	740 hp at 8,250 rpm
Maximum torque:	509 lb-ft (70.4 kgm) at 6,000 rpm
Valve actuation:	Twin overhead camshafts per bank
Valves:	Four per cylinder

Fuel feed:	Direct electronic fuel injection
Ignition:	Static electronic, multi-spark function
Cooling:	Water-cooled
Lubrication:	Dry sump

TRANSMISSION

Drive:	Rear-wheel drive
Clutch:	Dual
Gearbox:	Dual-clutch (DCT), 7-speed + reverse

CHASSIS

Bodywork:	Two-seater berlinetta

Frame:	Aluminum space frame		Front/rear track:	65.6/63.7 in (1,665/1,618 mm)
Front suspension:	Independent, double wishbones, coil springs, telescopic shock absorbers, anti-roll bar		Length:	181.8 in (4,618 mm)
			Width:	76.5 in (1,942 mm)
Rear suspension:	Independent, multilink, coil springs, telescopic shock absorbers, anti-roll bar		Height:	50.1 in (1,273 mm)
			Weight:	3,362 lb (1,525 kg)
Steering:	Rack and pinion		Fuel tank capacity:	24 gal (92 liters)
Front/rear brakes:	Carbon-ceramic discs			
Wheels:	20-in light alloy rims with 255/35 (front) and 315/35 (rear) tires			

DIMENSIONS AND WEIGHT

PERFORMANCE

Wheelbase:	107.1 in (2,720 mm)		Top speed:	Over 211 mph (340 km/h)
			Acceleration 0 to 60 mph (0 to 100 km/h):	3.1 seconds
			Weight/power ratio:	4.54 lb/hp (2.06 kg/hp)

FERRARI 458 SPECIALE

2013

Special by name and special by nature, the Speciale is an evolution of the 458 Italia offering extreme thrill and a specification with some astronomical figures. Starting with the specific power output of 2.21 hp/cu in (135 hp/l), the highest ever achieved by a naturally aspirated, road-going Ferrari, the car is packed with technological innovations designed to become the standard for the Ferraris of the future. This is the link between the present and the future. The power unit is a Maranello classic, a 32-valve 90° V8, the same as that fitted in the 458 Italia. It has a flat crankshaft, dry-sump lubrication, displacement of 275 cu in (4.5 liters), and many features transferred from competition experience.

Race technology, combined with direct fuel injection and variable timing on both the intake and the exhaust sides, give the Speciale a maximum power output of 605 hp and a torque of 399 lb-ft (55.1 kgm), compared with the 570 hp and 398 lb-ft (55 kgm) of the standard 458 engine. The car has been made considerably lighter and consequently weighs 198 lb (90 kg) less than the 458 Italia. This slimming-down allows the 458 Speciale to accelerate from 0 to 60 mph (0 to 100 km/h) in 3.0 seconds, four tenths of a second quicker than the model from which it derives.

The car features advances in active aerodynamics. Mobile flaps at the front and rear balance downforce and drag. Electronically controlled car setup makes high-performance driving easier. These are all technical features which make the 458 Speciale the series Ferrari with the highest lateral acceleration ever: 1.33 g.

TECHNICAL DATA

ENGINE

Type:	Central, longitudinal
Cylinders:	V8 (90°)
Bore x stroke:	3.70 x 3.19 in (94.0 x 81.0 mm)
Displacement:	275 cu in (4,499 cc)
Maximum power:	605 hp at 9,000 rpm
Maximum torque:	399 lb-ft (55.1 kgm) at 6,000 rpm
Valve actuation:	Twin overhead camshafts per bank
Valves:	Four per cylinder
Fuel feed:	Direct electronic fuel injection
Ignition:	Static electronic, one spark plug per cylinder
Cooling:	Water-cooled
Lubrication:	Dry sump

TRANSMISSION

Drive:	Rear-wheel drive
Clutch:	Dual
Gearbox:	Dual-clutch (DCT), 7-speed + reverse

CHASSIS

Bodywork:	Two-seater berlinetta
Frame:	Aluminum space frame
Front suspension:	Independent, double wishbones, coil springs, telescopic shock absorbers, anti-roll bar

Rear suspension:	Independent, multilink, coil springs, telescopic shock absorbers, anti-roll bar
Steering:	Rack and pinion
Front/rear brakes:	Carbon-ceramic discs
Wheels:	20-in light alloy rims with 245/35 (front) and 305/30 (rear) tires

DIMENSIONS AND WEIGHT

| Wheelbase: | 104.3 in (2,650 mm) |
| Front/rear track: | 66.1/64.3 in (1,679/1,632 mm) |

Length:	180.0 in (4,571 mm)
Width:	76.8 in (1,951 mm)
Height:	47.4 in (1,203 mm)
Weight:	2844 lb (1,290 kg)
Fuel tank capacity:	23 gal (86 liters)

PERFORMANCE

Top speed:	Over 202 mph (325 km/h)
Acceleration 0 to 60 mph (0 to 100 km/h):	3.0 seconds
Weight/power ratio:	4.70 lb/hp (2.13 kg/hp)

FERRARI SERGIO PININFARINA

2013

TECHNICAL DATA

ENGINE

Type:	Central, longitudinal
Cylinders:	V8 (90°)
Bore x stroke:	3.70 x 3.19 in (94.0 x 81.0 mm)
Displacement:	275 cu in (4,499 cc)
Maximum power:	570 hp at 9,000 rpm
Maximum torque:	398 lb-ft (55.0 kgm) at 6,000 rpm
Valve actuation:	Twin overhead camshafts per bank
Valves:	Four per cylinder
Fuel feed:	Direct electronic fuel injection
Ignition:	Static electronic, one spark plug per cylinder
Cooling:	Water-cooled
Lubrication:	Dry sump

TRANSMISSION

Drive:	Rear-wheel drive
Clutch:	Dual
Gearbox:	Dual-clutch (DCT), 7-speed + reverse

CHASSIS

Bodywork:	Two-seater barchetta

Frame:	Aluminum space frame
Front suspension:	Independent, double wishbones, coil springs, telescopic shock absorbers, anti-roll bar
Rear suspension:	Independent, multilink, coil springs, telescopic shock absorbers, anti-roll bar
Steering:	Rack and pinion
Front/rear brakes:	Carbon-ceramic discs
Wheels:	20-in light alloy rims with 235/35 (front) and 295/35 (rear) tires

DIMENSIONS AND WEIGHT

Wheelbase:	104.3 in (2,650 mm)
Front/rear track:	—
Length:	179.1 in (4,550 mm)
Width:	76.4 in (1,940 mm)
Height:	44.9 in (1,140 mm)
Weight:	2,822 lb (1,280 kg)
Fuel tank capacity:	23 gal (86 liters)

PERFORMANCE

Top speed:	199 mph (320 km/h)
Acceleration 0 to 60 mph (0 to 100 km/h):	3.4 seconds
Weight/power ratio:	4.96 lb/hp (2.25 kg/hp)

Sergio Pininfarina was the man who led the Pininfarina coachbuilder and design house for 40 years, styling and evolving the look of many legendary Ferraris. This concept car was presented at the Geneva International Motor Show in 2013 and is a two-seater barchetta commemorating the senator for life, the late Sergio Pininfarina, who had passed away just the year before.

The car was a design exercise based on a 458 spider, restating some of the styling elements of the Maranello roadsters of the nineteen-sixties and nineteen-seventies. It was, however, very much a concept car, an open top eliminating the retractable hardtop of the series vehicle in favor of . . . two crash helmets, for the driver and the passenger. This was necessary because the car, a true barchetta, had no windshield, substituted in this case by a deflector directing the flow of air upward. The roll bar protecting the cabin had a wing-shaped profile, an aerodynamic feature adding some extra down-force. The adoption of some radical solutions on the bodywork saw the weight drop from 3,153 lb for the 458 Spider to 2,822 lb (1,430 kg to 1,280 kg). This 331 lb (150 kg) weight reduction, combined with a powerful V8, meant that the car now did 0 to 60 mph (0 to 100 km/h) in 3.4 seconds instead of the 3.5 seconds for the series vehicle. The engine was a 275 cu in (4.5 liter) V8 with direct injection and variable timing, delivering 570 hp and fitted with a dual-clutch, 7-speed gearbox. The concept car had the same top speed of 199 mph (320 km/h).

FERRARI LaFERRARI

2013

TECHNICAL DATA

ENGINE

Type:	Central, longitudinal
Cylinders:	V12 (65°)
Bore x stroke:	3.70 x 2.96 in (94.0 x 75.2 mm)
Displacement:	382 cu in (6,262 cc)
Maximum power:	963 hp (combined)
Maximum torque:	664-ft (91.8 kgm) (combined)
Valve actuation:	Twin overhead camshafts per bank
Valves:	Four per cylinder
Fuel feed:	Direct electronic fuel injection
Ignition:	Static electronic, multi-spark function
Cooling:	Water-cooled
Lubrication:	Dry sump

TRANSMISSION

Drive:	Rear-wheel drive
Clutch:	Dual
Gearbox:	Dual-clutch (DCT), 7-speed + reverse

CHASSIS

Bodywork:	Two-seater berlinetta
Frame:	Carbon-fiber monocoque
Front suspension:	Independent, double wishbones, coil springs, telescopic shock absorbers, anti-roll bar
Rear suspension:	Independent, multilink, coil springs, telescopic shock absorbers, anti-roll bar
Steering:	Rack and pinion
Front/rear brakes:	Carbon-ceramic discs
Wheels:	Front: 19-in alloy rims with 265/30 tires
	Rear: 20-in alloy rims with 345/30 tires

DIMENSIONS AND WEIGHT

Wheelbase:	104.3 in (2,650 mm)
Front/rear track:	—
Length:	185.1 in (4,702 mm)
Width:	78.4 in (1,992 mm)
Height:	43.4 in (1,116 mm)
Weight:	est. 2,767 lb (1,255 kg)
Fuel tank capacity:	—

PERFORMANCE

Top speed:	Over 217 mph (350 km/h)
Acceleration 0 to 60 mph (0 to 100 km/h):	< 3.0 seconds
Weight/power ratio:	est. 2.87 lb/hp (1.30 kg/hp)

The forerunners of this car are the F40, the F50, and the Enzo. Only 499 examples will be built of the LaFerrari, the first series production hybrid with the Prancing Horse badge. This is extreme like no other berlinetta from Maranello and sees the debut of Formula 1 HY-KERS technology on a road car. HY-KERS takes the well-known 382 cu in (6,262 cc) V12 of the F12 Berlinetta developed to deliver 800 hp and an astonishing 9,250 rpm and combines it with a 163 hp electric motor.

This combination provides huge power and torque values (963 hp and 91.8 kgm), which allow it to get from 0 to 60 mph (0 to 100 km/h) in less than 3.0 seconds and have a top speed in excess of 217 mph (350 km/h).

Performance figures of this level are the result of keeping the weight down to 2,767 lb (1,255 kg) by incorporating the main electrical unit into the 7-speed, dual-clutch gearbox and introducing other technical refinements. The battery, weighing 132 lb (60 kg), is integrated into the carbon-fiber monocoque and charged by regenerative braking and the V12 itself when it is not running under load. The center of gravity is 1.4 in (35 mm) lower than that of the Enzo. The flat undertray is one of the benefits transferred from F1 experience. Active aerodynamics adapts the spoiler, extractor, and splitter profiles to vehicle speed in order to vary downforce in real time. This is the closest any current production car has come to being a Formula 1 vehicle.

FERRARI 488 GTB

2015

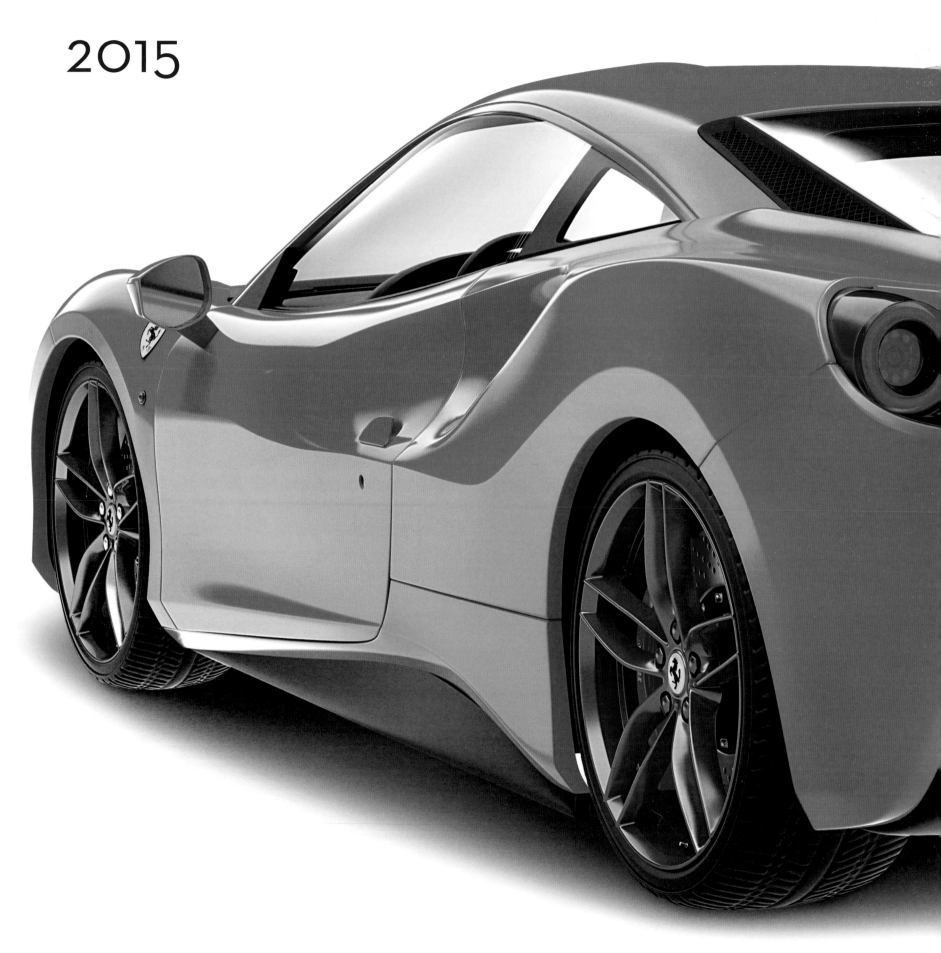

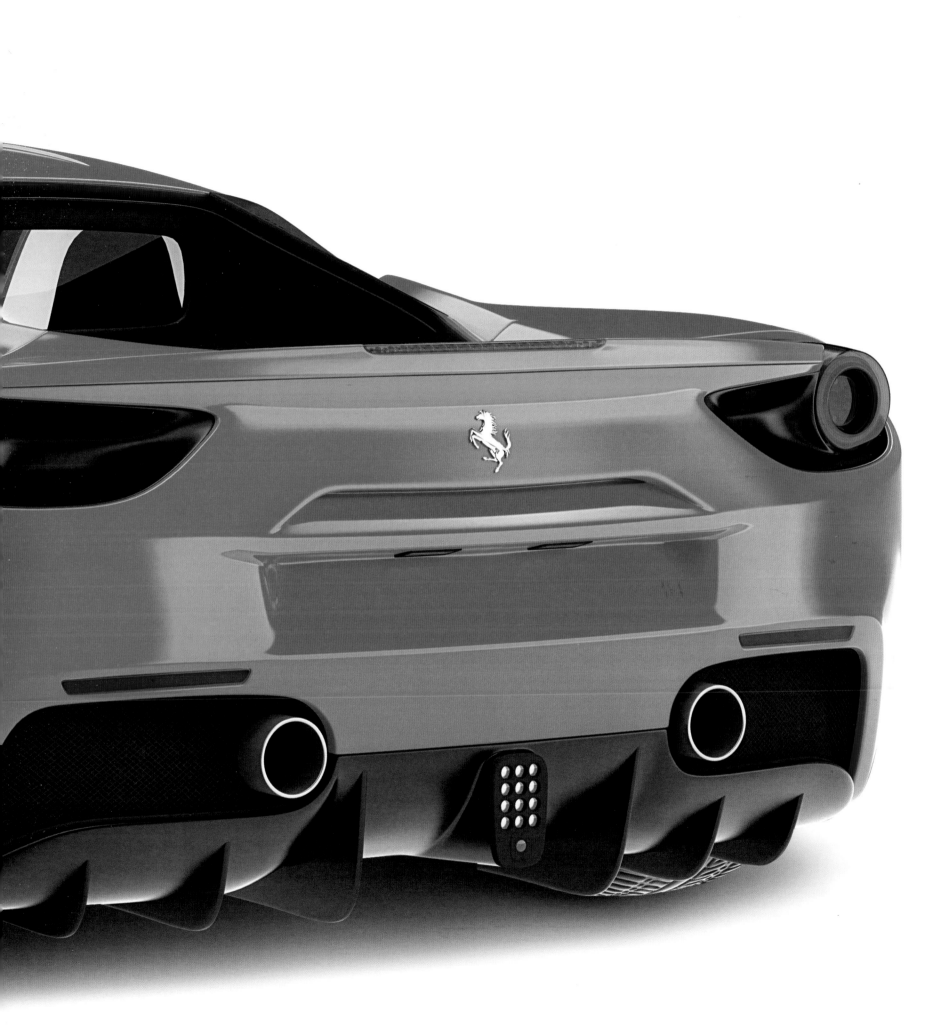

The 488 GTB represented a turning point in the history of road Ferraris in its return to supercharging, which had been abandoned by the F40 of 1987 to reduce emissions and fuel consumption. The sound and the capacity to increase revolutions of the 458 were slightly reduced, but the gain in power, torque, and effectiveness were seen to be such that everyone accepted it. Designed by Flavio Manzoni's Centro Stile Ferrari, the 488 differed from the 458 in the sculpture of the sides, with air ducts inspired by the 308 GTB that, forty years before, had "founded" the Ferrari family with the V8 rear-mounted engine.

It had 660.5 hp (670 cv), 100 more than the 458, but at 8,000 rpm instead of 9,000 rpm, and the specific power of 172 hp/liter (cv/l) set a new record for road Ferraris. The maximum torque increased from 398 lb/ft (55 kgm) at 6,000 rpm to 560.5 lb/ft (77.5 kgm) at 3,000 rpm, with very evident advantages for drivability. The extremely sophisticated tuning of the supercharger practically eliminated any delay in response to the accelerator.

Thanks to experience in competition, the downforce was over 50% above that of the 458, reaching 716 lb (325 kg) at 155 mph (250 km/h). As far as management of the driving dynamics was concerned, the 488 embodied a ride control (Side Slip Control—SSC2) that was more precise and less intrusive, which analyzed different parameters to enable longitudinal acceleration that was greater by 12% when leaving curves. The SSC2 made use of F1-trac traction control, the electronic differential E-diff, and the active damping of the shock absorbers.

TECHNICAL DATA

ENGINE

Type:	Central, longitudinal
Cylinders:	V8 (90°)
Bore x stroke:	3.4 x 3.3 in (86.5 x 83.0 mm)
Displacement:	3,902 cc
Maximum power:	660.5 hp (670 cv) at 8,000 rpm
Maximum torque:	560.5 lb/ft (77.5 kgm) at 3,000 rpm
Valve activation:	Double overhead camshaft
Valves:	4 per cylinder
Fuel feed:	Bosch MED17.3.5 electronic injection, two IHI/ Honeywell turbos with intercooler
Ignition:	Bosch single, static electronic MED17.3.5
Cooling:	Water-cooled
Lubrication:	Dry sump

TRANSMISSION

Drive:	Rear-wheel drive
Clutch:	Dual
Gearbox:	F1 7-speed dual-clutch + reverse

CHASSIS

Bodywork:	Two-seater berlinetta
Frame:	Aluminum space-frame
Front suspension:	Independent double wishbones, coil springs, magnetorheological telescopic shock absorbers
Rear suspension:	Independent double wishbones, coil springs, magnetorheological telescopic shock absorbers
Steering:	Pinion and rack-and-pinion
Front/rear brakes:	Self-ventilating disc
Wheels:	20-in alloy rims with front tires 245/35 and rear tires 305/30

DIMENSIONS AND WEIGHT

Wheelbase:	104.3 in (2,650 mm)
Front/rear track:	66.1/64.8 in (1,679/1,647 mm)
Length:	179.8 in (4,568 mm)
Width:	76.9 in (1,952 mm)
Height:	47.8 in (1,213 mm)
Weight:	3020 lb (1,370 kg)
Fuel tank capacity:	20 gal (78 liters)

PERFORMANCE

Top speed:	205 mph (330 km/h)
Acceleration 0-60 mph (0-100 km/h):	3.0 seconds
Weight/power ratio:	359.46 kW/tonne

FERRARI
F12TDF

2015

The F12 was created in 2012 to replace the 599 in the role of flagship car of the front-mounted-engine range. However, in 2015, Ferrari presented the tdf in a limited edition (799 cars), which was higher performance and more evocative. The name tdf was an abbreviation of Tour de France, a race in stages that Ferrari won thirteen times between 1951 and 1982. The V12 of 6.3 liters, the same as the "normal" F12, increased from 730 hp (740 cv) to 770 hp (780 cv).

The top speed remained unchanged (over 211 mph), but the accel-

eration improved, and to go from 0 to 124 mph (0 to 200 km/h), only 7.9 sec were required instead of 8.5. The body was characterized by added air intakes on the hood and on the rear mudguards (the latter inspired by those of the legendary 250 GTO). It used wider front tires and wheel tracks than the standard F12 and had a different aerodynamic configuration due to the larger front spoiler and different positioning of the rear spoiler, which was 2.3 in (60 mm) farther back and 1.2 in (30 mm) higher. All this made it possible to increase the down-force by 87% (507 lb at 124 mph), taking it to an unprecedented level for a road car. However, the most important mechanical novelty was the Passo Corto Virtuale (PCV), a system that enabled the rear wheels to steer together with the front wheels (but at much smaller angles) to improve stability at high speeds.

The weight was decreased by 242 lb (110 kg) after a thorough review of the body, interior, engine, transmission, and mechanics, and with the extensive use of composite materials.

TECHNICAL DATA

ENGINE

Type:	Front, longitudinal
Cylinders:	V12 (65°)
Bore x stroke:	3.7 x 2.96 in (94 x 75.{{2 mm)
Displacement:	6,262 cc
Maximum power:	770 hp (780 cv) at 8,500 rpm
Maximum torque:	520 lb/ft (71.9 kgm) at 6,250 rpm
Valve actuation:	Double overhead camshaft
Valves:	4 per cylinder
Fuel feed:	Electronic ignition

Ignition:	Single, static electronic
Cooling:	Water-cooled
Lubrication:	Dry-sump

TRANSMISSION

Drive:	Rear-wheel drive
Clutch:	Double
Gearbox:	F1 7-speed dual-clutch + reverse gear

CHASSIS

Bodywork:	Two-seater berlinetta
Frame:	Aluminum space-frame

Front suspension:	Independent double wishbones, coil springs, magnetorheological telescopic shock absorbers
Rear suspension:	Independent double wishbones, coil springs, magnetorheological telescopic shock absorbers
Steering:	Pinion and rack-and-pinion
Front/rear brakes:	Carbon-ceramic disc
Wheels:	20-in alloy rims with front tires 275/35 and rear tires 315/35

DIMENSIONS AND WEIGHT

Wheelbase:	107.1 in (2,720 mm)
Front/rear track:	65.9/63.7 in (1,673/1,648 mm)
Length:	183.3 in (4,656 mm)
Width:	77.2 in (1,961 mm)
Height:	50.1 in (1,273 mm)
Weight:	3119.5 lb (1,415 kg)
Fuel tank capacity:	24.3 gal (92 liters)

PERFORMANCE

Top speed:	over 211 mph (340 km/h)
Acceleration 0-60 mph (0-100 km/h):	2.9 seconds
Weight/power ratio:	405.52 kW/tonne

FERRARI SF90 STRADALE

2019

The name SF90 is the same one used for the F1 one-seater created for the 2019 world championships. The reason for this choice was the adoption of a power unit inspired by that of the racing car. The heat engine derived from that of the F8 Tributo, but its power increased from 710 to 770 hp (720 to 780 cv) and it was assisted by three electric engines: one at the rear and two at the front (one for each wheel to optimize the stability), which in total developed 216 hp (220 cv). Therefore, in all, the car in the most extreme functioning mode, "Qualify," had

986 hp (1,000 cv), at that time the highest ever for a road Ferrari. The arrangement of the engines made this car, to all intents and purposes, a four-wheel drive. The lithium batteries could also be charged from outside and enabled the SF90 Stradale to reach 84 mph (135 km/h) in electric-only mode and to travel at "zero emissions" for about 25 km. But it was in full-power mode that the performance was outstanding: over 211 mph (340 km/h), 2.5 sec from 0 to 62 mph (0 to 100 km/h) and 6.7 sec to reach 124 mph (200 km/h). The aerodynamics could only be highly evolved: winged profiles and highly sophisticated air channels and even "helical" wheel rims which extracted air from under the shell to increase the ground effect. The result was a record ground force: 860 lb (390 kg) of supplementary force at 155 mph (250 km/h). The SF90 Stradale was also a "groundbreaking" car on an aesthetic level, because it had unusual external proportions (the cockpit was forward and low, the nose was short, the tail was low and long) and an unprecedented completely digital instrument panel.

TECHNICAL DATA

HEAT ENGINE

Placing:	Rear, longitudinal
Cylinders:	V8 (90°)
Bore x stroke:	3.46 x 3.23 in (88.0 x 82.0 mm)
Displacement:	3,990 cc
Maximum power:	770 hp (780 cv) at 7,500 rpm
Maximum torque:	590 lb/ft (81.5 kgm) at 6,000 rpm
Valve actuation:	Double overhead camshaft
Valves:	4 per cylinder
Fuel feed:	Electronic injection, two IHI/Honeywell turbos with intercooler

Ignition:	Single, static electronic
Cooling:	Water-cooled
Lubrication:	Dry-sump

ELECTRIC ENGINES

Placing:	2 front, 1 rear
Maximum power:	162 kW (216 hp)
Battery capacity:	7.9 kWh

TRANSMISSION

Drive:	Four-wheel
Clutch:	Dual-plate
Gearbox:	F1 8 speed dual-clutch + reverse gear

CHASSIS

Bodywork:	Two-seater berlinetta
Frame:	Aluminum space-frame
Front suspension:	Independent double wishbones, coil springs, magnetorheological telescopic shock absorbers, anti-roll bar
Rear suspension:	Independent double wishbones, coil springs, magnetorheological telescopic shock absorbers, anti-roll bar
Steering:	Pinion and rack-and-pinion
Front/rear brakes:	Carbon-ceramic disc
Wheels:	20-in alloy rims with front tires 255/35 and rear tires 315/30

DIMENSIONS AND WEIGHT

Wheelbase:	104.3 in (2,650 mm)
Front/rear track:	66.1/65 in (1,679/1,652 mm)
Length:	185.4 in (4,710 mm)
Width:	77.6 in (1,972 mm)
Height:	46.7 in (1,186 mm)
Weight:	3,461 lb (1,570 kg)
Fuel tank capacity:	18 gal (68 liters)

PERFORMANCE

Top speed:	over 211 mph (340 km/h)
Acceleration 0-60 mph (0-100 km/h):	2.5 seconds
Weight/power ratio:	365.25 kW/tonne

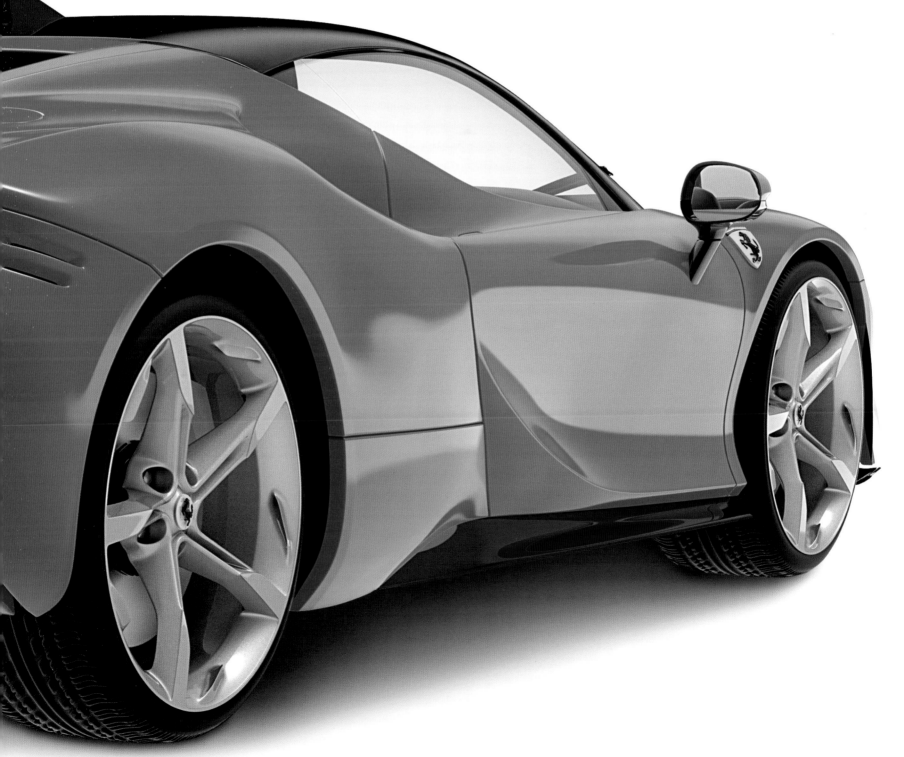

Photo Credits

Text

SAVERIO VILLA HAS ALWAYS WORKED IN THE FIELD OF AUTOMOBILE JOURNALISM. AS A FAN OF BOTH MODERN AND VINTAGE CARS, HE TRANSFORMED HIS HOBBY INTO A CAREER IN 1985. HE HAS EDITED THE PRINT PUBLICATIONS *EVO, AUTO OGGI,* AND *PANORAMAUTO* AND WRITTEN FOR *AUTO, AM, AUTOSPRINT, GENTE MOTORI, AUTOMOBILISMO, AL VOLANTE* AND *AUTO TECNICA.*

NOWADAYS HE CONTRIBUTES TO *YOUNGTIMER, RUOTECLASSICHE, TOPGEAR, CORRIERE DELLA SERA,* AND *AUTOMOBILE CLUB D'ITALIA.* HE HAS WRITTEN NUMEROUS BOOKS ON THE HISTORY OF THE AUTOMOBILE AND WAS EDITORIAL DIRECTOR OF THE TELEVISION PROGRAM *YELLOW MOTORI* AND CONSULTANT FOR THE ITALIAN EDITION OF *TOPGEAR.* FOR WHITE STAR PUBLISHERS HE HAS WRITTEN THE VOLUMES *FERRARI: THE LEGENDARY MODELS* AND *LEGENDARY CONVERTIBLES* (WITH MARCO COLETTO).

Rendering

MARCO DE FABIANIS MANFERTO, INDUSTRIAL DESIGNER, HOLDS A MASTER IN PRODUCT DESIGN FROM ISTITUTO EUROPEO DI DESIGN (IED). HE SPECIALIZED IN 3D MODELING AT THE POLITECNICO DI MILANO. FOR WHITE STAR PUBLISHERS HE HAS UNDERTAKEN THE "RENDERING" OF VARIOUS BOOKS IN PRESTIGIOUS SERIES. HE HAS ALSO WORKED AS EDITORIAL CONSULTANT FOR THE SERIES ON MUSIC PUBLISHED BY WHITE STAR AND IN PARTICULAR WAS THE EDITOR OF THE TITLE *HEAVY METAL.*

Project editor

VALERIA MANFERTO DE FABIANIS

Editorial coordination

GIORGIA RAINERI

Graphic design

MARIA CUCCHI

WS White Star Publishers® is a registered trademark property of White Star s.r.l.

© 2020 White Star s.r.l.
Piazzale Luigi Cadorna, 6
20123 Milan, Italy
www.whitestar.it

Translation: Arancho Doc—Iceigeo, Milan (Jonathan West and Katherine Clifton)

ISBN 978-88-544-1672-7
2 3 4 5 6 26 25 24 23 22

Printed in Serbia

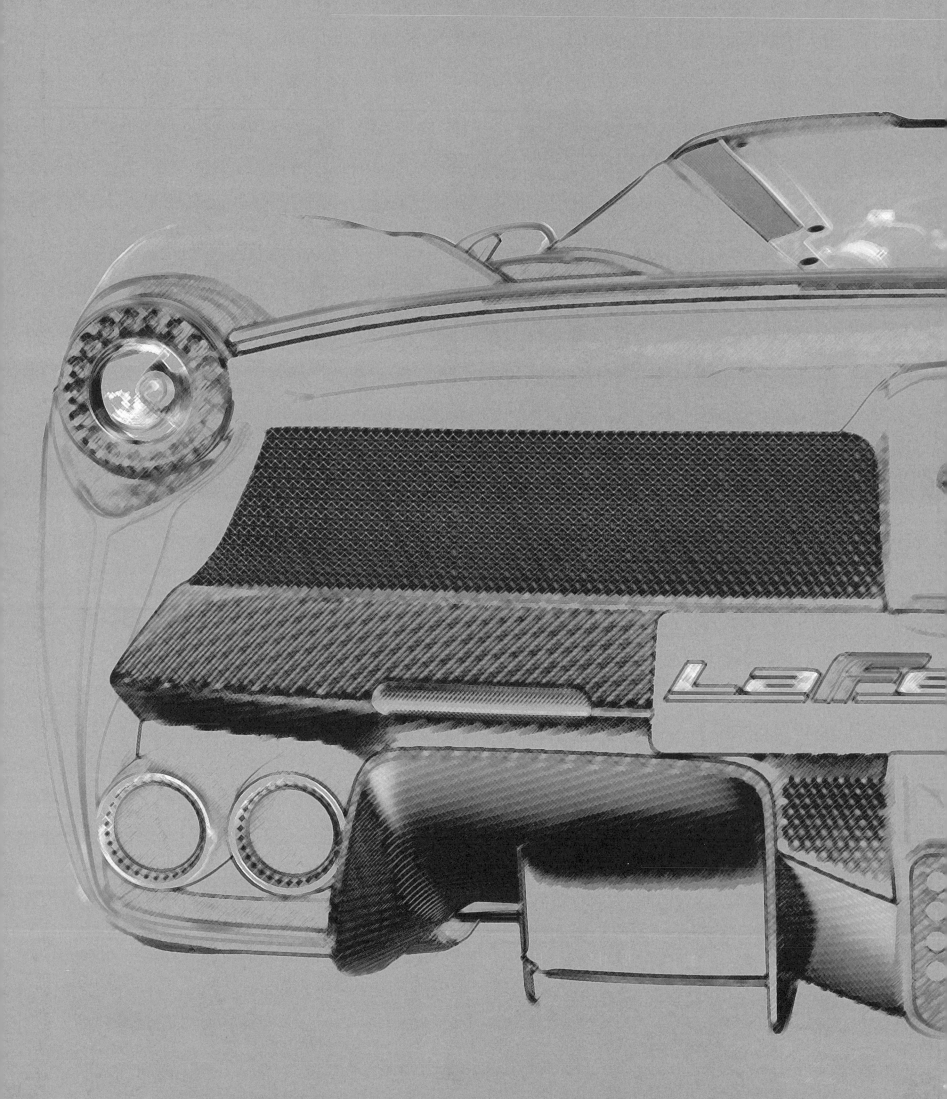